Praise for *The Path of* ⁙‖‖‖‖‖‖‖‖‖‖‖‖‖‖‖

C000068832

"An exquisite and profound unfolding of Jewish mysticism with inviting practices that reveal deep truth."

—Jack Kornfield, PhD, author of *A Path With Heart*

"Zvi Ish-Shalom is an important leader for our time. He is not only a Kabbalah scholar but he is also connected to divine wisdom which emanates throughout the pages of this book. Zvi helps us understand that all parts of us are divine and valuable no matter how they contract us; and how we can access our eternal, true self and its light. I know him to be a man who walks his talk, and through this book he invites us to join him on the journey to freedom that he embodies."

—Richard C. Schwartz, PhD, developer of the Internal Family Systems model and author of *No Bad Parts*

"In language of luminous clarity and brilliant power, *The Path of Primordial Light* transmits the blessings and energies of a sacred world. A magical book."

—Gaylon Ferguson, PhD, author of *Natural Wakefulness*

"With penetrating intelligence, and the confidence born from direct experience, Zvi Ish-Shalom is almost single-handedly bringing the deepest wisdom of Jewish mysticism into modern life. *The Path of Primordial Light* is a masterpiece of cultural translation, sure to benefit anyone fortunate enough to encounter it. Surrender to the radical simplicity of his message."

—Andrew Holecek, author of *Dreams of Light:*
The Profound Daytime Practice of Lucid Dreaming.

"With his unique combination of skills, the Rabbi-scholar-contemplative-mystic, Zvi Ish-Shalom is uniquely qualified to reanimate the deep mystical heart of his beloved Jewish tradition. And that's just what he does in this accessible yet profound book, which offers a path and practices pointing Jewish (and other) contemplatives to the bottomless depths and gifts of this ancient tradition."

—Roger Walsh, MD, PhD, author of *Essential Spirituality:*
The Seven Central Practices

THE PATH OF PRIMORDIAL LIGHT

ANCIENT WISDOM FOR THE HERE AND NOW

ZVI ISH-SHALOM

Light Beacon Press
5013 S Louise Ave
Suite 572
Sioux Falls, SD 57108

Library of Congress Cataloging-In-Publication Data

Names: Ish-Shalom, Zvi, author.
Title: The path of primordial light: ancient wisdom for the here and now
/ Zvi Ish-Shalom.
Description: Sioux Falls, South Dakota: Light Beacon Press, [2022]

Identifiers:
ISBN 9798985874105 (paperback)
ISBN 979-8-9858741-1-2 (epub)

Subjects: LCSH: Mysticism--Judaism. | Cabala. | Religious awakening--
Judaism. | Spiritual healing--Judaism. | Peace of mind--Religious
aspects--Judaism.

Classification: LCC BM723.I84 2022
(paperback)| LCC BM723.I84 (ebook)
| DDC 296.712--dc23

Library of Congress Control Number: 2022906546

Cover Design: Zvi Ish-Shalom
Book Layout: Light Beacon Press
Copyediting: Audra Figgins and Isaiah Friedman

CONTENTS

INTRODUCTION

This book is about the primordial light that illuminates all of creation. Specifically, it is a manual that will help you understand and experience this light in an ongoing way.

I first experienced this light while practicing the traditional Judaism of my childhood. As this experience deepened, I began to perceive what felt like vast, endless, and nondimensional realms of primordial light. After many years of integrating these experiences, I shared a body of teachings and practices with a group of students that elucidated the mystical heart of Judaism from the perspective of this primordial light. I called these teachings Kedumah (which in Hebrew means "primordial"), or the Path of Primordial Light.

Kedumah draws from ancient Hebrew mysticism and applies universal contemplative methods to support people from all religions, backgrounds, and cultures to experience the primordial light directly and to embody it in their everyday life. In this book, I share some of the core principles and practices of this Path of Primordial Light.

The main goal of this book is to facilitate an experiential shift of consciousness. As such, while we will be learning many metaphysical concepts and principles, they are not primarily meant to be intellectual exercises. Rather, they are pointers to the experience of presence and beyond, to more hidden dimensions of reality that cannot be known by the conventional mind.

For this reason, in this book I will not be providing formal citations of my textual sources, so that you can pay more attention to your inner experience and the innate wisdom that arises from within. If you wish to examine in greater depth the traditional sources for many of the teachings that I reference, please consult my book, *The Kedumah Experience: The Primordial Torah*, which contains extensive textual documentation.

Since the main goal of this book is to facilitate an experiential shift of consciousness and to share a step-by-step set of practices, it will be most effective if you read from a place of presence and inner connection. By *presence* I mean the embodied and palpable experience of "is-ness", or of simply being, that is present when we are not identified with our thinking mind.

One simple way to connect with presence is to take a conscious breath. You can try this right now. Take a few full breaths and as you breathe out each time, allow your thinking mind to release and dissolve. Notice what it's like to just be here right now without thoughts. In this state of "just being" without thinking, notice what you experience, what you feel. See if you can drop more into this feeling mode as you read, sensing the energetic vibrations of the letters on the page as well as the palpable space that is present in the spaces between the letters and words.

As you read this book, consider pausing occasionally to take a few breaths and practice being present in the here and now, even if it's just for a few moments. As much as possible, be aware of your experience, noticing how you are impacted by the teachings. I recommend that you take some time to reflect on your experience of each chapter before you move on to the next one. You can also keep a journal of your process, or even better, find a spiritual friend to read this book with you so you can share and unpack your experiences together.

I appreciate you taking the time to join me on this journey.

May it bring you many blessings.

CHAPTER 1

THE PRIMORDIAL LIGHT

I n the ancient Hebrew tradition, the word *Kedumah* means "primordial" or "ancient." Mystically speaking, this term refers to the cosmic source of creation, to the hidden light that illuminates all of reality.

In an ancient compendium of Jewish lore called the Midrash, it states: "When the Holy One created the world, He consulted the Torah and created the world". Here, the word *Torah* does not refer to the literal Bible. Rather, it refers to the Primordial Torah, the *Torah Kedumah*. The Primordial Torah is the cosmic blueprint of creation, the original light that patterns all of existence.

Indeed, even the word *Torah*, which literally means "teaching," is understood by the ancient mystics to be a code word for this hidden light. This is why the book of Proverbs states, "Torah is light." The real Torah is thus not a book, a religion, or a set of doctrines or beliefs. Real Torah is the primordial light itself.

In the ancient mystical text known as the Zohar, this principle is further clarified. It states: "The Holy One gazed into the Torah, and created the world". Here, the Torah is a primordial portal through which the divine mystery gazes and manifests the world of form, the world of appearances. If we can understand how this process works, how the infinite becomes finite, then we can also learn how to return back to the source and experience our infinite and formless nature.

According to the book of Genesis, the human being is created in the image of God (*Elohim* in Hebrew). In the Kabbalah, this divine name does not refer to a transcendent entity but rather to all manifest reality. This means that every individual is a microcosm of the totality, an earthly expression of the divine body that encompasses the entire universe.

This is why the Talmud states, "one who destroys a single life destroys the entire universe". Since the human being embodies the full spectrum of light that constitutes all of reality, each one of us is a microcosm of the manifest God, a unique expression of the primordial blueprint of creation.

This principle is implicit in the Zohar's teaching that the Holy One gazed into the Torah and created the world. It points to the potential for the human being to gaze through the portal of primordial light from the opposite direction, from the perspective of a finite human being. Just as the Holy One gazed into the primordial light to create the world, we too have the potential to move from the finite to the infinite, to experience ourselves as the benevolent light that animates all of existence.

The Path of Primordial Light teaches us how to gaze through this primordial portal to perceive our formless, infinite nature, and it also shows us how to step fully into the world to manifest our infinite nature in the finite realm of creation. The fulfillment of our human potential thus includes both the realization of our formless nature as well as our embodiment into physical form, as a unique individual cell of the cosmic body—one that cannot be duplicated by anyone else. So, this path guides us to experience the divine light that transcends time and space, and then helps us to embody this light in our mundane day-to-day life.

The primordial light of creation is not something that only existed long ago in linear time. It is always-already present in the here and now. It is the very ground of our experience in each and every moment. The hidden portal of primordial light abides deep in the core of our being; it silently awaits us beneath all of our thoughts and concepts. It reveals itself to us in the spacious ground of stillness and peace that fills the spaces between the letters and words that you are reading right now. Notice these spaces and turn toward them. Drop into them and notice what arises.

CHAPTER 2

THE FIVE JOURNEYS

The spiritual journey calls us to shift our perception, to alter the way that we experience reality. If we travel from one place on earth to another, we don't need to change at all. At most, we may need to change our clothing depending on the weather outside and where we are traveling to. But the spiritual journey is about changing into an altogether different kind of person—a person who is no longer locked inside the historically conditioned mind.

Therefore, for a spiritual teaching to work, it requires that we engage the path with our totality, not just with our thinking minds. Philosophies, ideologies, science, and theories can be understood only with the thinking mind. Spiritual teachings, however, require a much more complete understanding, one that includes the wisdom of our head, heart, body, and soul. In Kedumah, this more integral journey of transformation is marked by five distinct stages or landmarks. We call them the *five journeys*, and they are contraction, expansion, wholeness, vastness, and freedom.

The five journeys serve as prototypes for the transformation of our consciousness. They ultimately can help guide us toward greater inner freedom. This freedom allows us to be fully who and what we are, to be alive as a human finite form in a manner that is totally connected to, and inseparable from, the infinite source.

In order to understand how the five journeys can be utilized on the spiritual journey, let us compare them to a sacred scroll. Sacred scrolls are revered not because of the interesting stories they contain, but because they serve as vehicles for the hidden light of presence, the primordial light.

There are four levels to a sacred scroll, each one corresponding with a specific dimension of the human being. The words of the scroll, and in particular the way the words combine to form narratives, correlate with the garments that we wear; the individual letters of the scroll correlate with the body; the ink corresponds with the presence that animates the body; and the blank parchment correlates with the nonconceptual primordial light, our innermost nature.

These four levels of the scroll and their human parallels correspond with the five journeys. The first journey, that of contraction, is the level of the conceptual narratives, the garments. They are the stories that constitute our sense of self-identity. The journey of expansion is the level of the body—the individual letters inscribed upon the scroll, the embodiments of our unique forms of light. The journey of wholeness corresponds with the spirit that animates the body and the ink that inscribes the individual letter. The journey of vastness corresponds to the blank parchment or the primordial light at the core of our being. And finally, the journey of freedom corresponds with the all-inclusive totality of the scroll itself: the blank parchment, ink, letters, and words that form the narratives. As such, the journey of freedom corresponds to the totality of the human being: our innermost primordial nature, the presence that animates us, our true body, and the conceptual narratives that form our self-identity.

In the coming chapters, we will unpack each of these journeys so that we can begin to appreciate how to utilize their wisdom toward the transformation of our perception and the awakening of our consciousness. However, before we move on to the next chapter, I want to invite you to pause for a moment and take a few conscious breaths. As you release each breath, allow your thinking mind to dissolve and drop into the presence of just being.

From this state of presence, consider reading this chapter again; but this time, instead of reading the letters and words as intellectual content, see what it's like to feel their energetic vibrations. What is it like to be touched by the inner essence of the letters as expressions of the primordial light?

CHAPTER 3

DIMENSIONS OF FREEDOM

T he five journeys represent different ways that the infinite experiences itself in the finite realm of creation. The first journey, contraction, which corresponds with the level of the garments, is the first thing we see when we gaze at the world. When we meet someone, perhaps the first thing we notice is the clothes they are wearing. This is the most surface layer of the human being, corresponding with the words of the scroll and the narratives—the stories—that these words form. Similarly, when we perceive objects in the world, we tend to notice their most superficial characteristics and immediately reify what we see with a conceptual label.

Thus, the journey of contraction represents the conventional mode of perception. It is marked by seeing ourselves and reality at the surface. In this mode, our range of perception is quite limited and contracted. This experience of contracted perception corresponds with the words and narratives of the scroll—they are the stories that constitute the surface layers of our experience. These stories are historically derived and crafted in response to our experiences as children. They are the garments that we wear. They are the material out of which we construct all of our self-images, identities, and narratives that define who we are and what reality is.

However, if you are reading this book, then you already know that there is something deeper than the garments. The body is a more real or true expression of what we are in our depth. This is not to suggest that there is anything wrong with the garments, stories, and narratives. However, in a certain way, the body is closer to our essence. When we meet someone and we see beneath the surface layer of their immediate appearance, we appreciate their unique individuality—we can see more clearly how they are a unique letter inscribed upon the scroll of reality. So, in this case, we're seeing something more real and true about them. It's more real and true because it's more of their totality; they are not just their garments, they are far more interesting than that.

The true body corresponds with the journey of expansion that represents a stage of the path where we expand beyond the confines of our contracted mode of perception into a more expansive experience of who we are and of what reality is. At this stage, we begin to experience the expansive light of presence, which comes with a greater sense of embodied freedom from the usual identity-dramas and thought-stories that typically confine us.

When we work through an experience of contraction and we understand the psychodynamic origins of the historical thought-stories associated with it, the light of presence can break through the contraction and we experience our bodies as more expansive and free.

As we deepen into this light of presence, the journey of wholeness, which corresponds with the ink that animates the letters of the scroll, begins to open. Wholeness represents the integration of the journeys of contraction and expansion.

In the usual situation, if we are able to effectively work with a contraction, it transforms into expansion. Then, we tend to experience the state of expansion in contrast to contraction: expansion feels good and we want it, while contraction feels bad and we don't want it. However, in the journey of wholeness, we recognize that the experience of contraction and expansion are two sides of the same coin and are ultimately inseparable.

This recognition and our acceptance of it brings with it a palpable sense of wholeness and completeness, and we experience a more full and robust embodiment of presence, of our essential substance, of the ink that animates our individual letter. In this journey, the light of presence that shines more freely through our bodies in the journey of expansion begins to integrate more fully into our ordinary everyday life. We begin to experience ourselves as the ink, the magical substance of presence itself.

But there's an even more subtle level: the blank parchment upon which all the words and all the letters are inscribed. According to the ancient Hebrew texts, the primordial Torah is written with black fire on white fire. The journey of vastness represents this white fire, the blank parchment that is the primordial formless ground of being itself, the nonconceptual source out of which all of reality arises. This is the dimension of the primordial light. As we learned in chapter 1, this is the interface between the infinite and the finite.

At this stage, we begin to experience the simplicity of *what is* when we are freed from the historically driven thinking mind altogether. As with the practice that we explored in the first chapter, when we take a full breath and drop into just being, we are inviting this experience of vastness. When we allow ourselves to just be present without identifying with the thinking mind at all, we are tasting the possibilities that the vastness of just being offers. Ultimately, the journey of vastness brings us to a condition in which there is no thinking or sense of self-identity whatsoever. We abide in the immaculate silence and stillness of deep peace.

The journey of vastness can then reveal to us the journey of freedom, which is an even more subtle truth. It's tricky to talk about because it is not a dimension of reality or an inner experience in the same way that the other journeys are. It's more the recognition of the radical singularity of all reality, whereby all particular expressions of the whole are nonhierarchically perceived. Everything that ever was, is, and will be is here recognized as equally valid expressions of the whole.

Freedom is thus a mode of experiencing in which the ordinary and the galactic are completely collapsed into each other, erasing all psychic investment in the content of our experience. It is a condition of radical freedom because there is no longer any searching or striving for any enlightenment or spiritual realization at all, because in this mode everything that is experienced—whether it be sublime, mundane, or even disturbing—inherently includes everything else within it. It is freedom because there is no impulse to seek something more ultimate or more meaningful than what is right in front of our faces at any moment in time.

The journey of freedom represents the primary view and orientation of Kedumah and is reflected in the statement from the most ancient Kabbalistic text, *The Book of Creation*, that "the end is embedded in the beginning and the beginning is embedded in the end." The equalization of beginning and end, of before and after, of above and below, of sacred and profane, of cosmic and ordinary, represents the radical nature of *Ein Sof*, the nonhierarchical "no end" of the Kabbalistic journey. In the Path of Primordial Light, we refer to this endless nature of reality as the journey of freedom.

So, pause for a moment and take a few full breaths. As you release each breath, allow your thinking mind to relax and dissolve. Drop into a state of presence—of just being. Notice what you experience right now. Remain here for a few moments, just being present and noticing what arises. From this state, try reading this chapter over again; but this time, instead of focusing on the black letters, become more aware of the white letters, the blank spaces between the letters and the words. What happens when you read in this manner? What do you notice and experience?

CHAPTER 4

THE BREATH OF LIFE

S o far, we have been practicing touching into presence by taking a conscious breath and relaxing and releasing the thinking mind. We have also been paying attention to the spaces between the words and letters. Through these practices, we are including more of what is here and now in our conscious awareness, in our experience. Usually, we are located inside the historically constructed stories and narratives of our thoughts, which are always grounded in some memory of the past or some anticipation of the future. But by consciously taking a full breath and relaxing our thinking mind, we are opening up to the possibility of experiencing what is actually present in the now.

In the ancient Hebrew tradition, the breath is what animates our consciousness. At the very beginning of the book of Genesis, in describing the creation of the human being, it states: "And He breathed into his nostrils the breath of life." This "breath of life" is the living soul, our consciousness. In fact, three different Hebrew words appear in the Torah to refer to the soul (*nefesh*, *ruach*, and *neshama*), and all of them are variations of words that mean "breath."

So, we see that the breath and the soul, both of which can only be experienced in the here and now, are intimately connected. That is why we can use the breath as a bridge to the experience of presence. Not only is it a very accessible portal to the here and now as breathing can only be experienced in the here and now, but it is also constituted by the material of consciousness itself, the breath of life. To experience this does not require hours of meditating on the breath. All it takes is a single moment of conscious awareness. All it takes is a single breath.

Let's explore this more deeply. There are two main ingredients to the breathing process. The first is the in-breath. As the breath flows in through our nostrils or mouth and fills our lungs, it animates our body with life. The second ingredient is the out-breath. As the breath is released from our system, our life force is released with it. Whenever we take a conscious breath, we are automatically shifting our awareness away from the thinking mind to the here and now, which is the only "place" where presence can be found. At the same time, by becoming conscious of our breath, we are becoming more aware of the substance and spirit of consciousness itself, the breath of life.

But there is also another dimension to the breathing process. At the very top of the in-breath, in between the in-breath and the out-breath, there is a gap, a pause, a space where there is no in-breath and no out-breath. Similarly, at the very bottom of the out-breath, there is a space, a gap, a pause where there is no in-breath and no out-breath. Once we get the knack of how to shift our awareness from the thinking mind to the here and now of the breath, we can try adding an awareness of these gaps, these spaces between the breaths.

You can try this right now. Take a full breath, hold it for a brief moment at the top of the in-breath, and then release the breath and hold it for a brief moment at the bottom of the out-breath. Stay present, aware, and awake in these spaces between the breaths. Try this one more time. Take a full breath, hold it for a brief moment at the top of the in-breath, and then release the breath and hold it for a brief moment at the bottom of the out-breath. Stay present, aware, and awake in these spaces between the breaths. Notice what it's like to be present in these in-between spaces.

Now let's explore this even further. Earlier in this book, I introduced the practice of becoming aware of the energetic vibrations of the letters and words, of the animating light that permeates them. I also introduced the practice of becoming aware of the spaces in between the letters and words. The letters and words, especially when they are articulated into speech, are simply extensions of the breath. The breath is what animates the letters and words with sound and articulates the sound into speech. Thus, the breath takes on more richness and dimensionality through its expression into sound and speech. Similarly, being aware of the spaces in between the words brings in the presence of stillness and formlessness.

With this experiential exploration, we are putting into practice the very first teachings of this book, contemplating the infinite, formless source of creation and its manifestation into the forms and expressions of the finite realm. The primordial light of creation is accessed through the spaces and gaps between our breaths and between the words of speech. The living presence of all the manifested forms of creation corresponds with the breath itself, the sounds and vibrations of our voice, and the letters and words inscribed upon the parchment of life.

The ancient Hebrew teachings correlate the human being to a Torah scroll. The blank parchment of formlessness parallels the empty spaces and gaps in-between the breath. The breath itself is the ink that animates the individual letter, which is our body. And articulating our breath into speech is the formation of the words of the scroll. So, we see that something as simple as taking a conscious breath can be a powerful way to shift our experience from one that is lost in thought to one that is more an expression of the totality of the human scroll that we are. This helps us become more grounded and connected to the union of formlessness and form, of the infinite and finite.

Before you move on to the next chapter, take some time to practice conscious breathing, noticing the animating life force of the breath as well as the infinite spaces of vastness between the breaths.

CHAPTER 5

TOTAL BEING

We have been exploring how the breath can serve as a bridge to presence. As the spirit that animates our consciousness in each moment, the breath is the life force not only of our individual experience but of creation itself. With each breath, we are born anew. According to the Hebrew mystics, everything that occurs in the human realm has a cosmic parallel. So, our earthly breathing reflects a cosmic process and can therefore be traced back to these primordial roots of existence, to the act of creation itself.

When we talk about creation, we usually think about it within a linear framework of time and space. Creation is usually thought to be something that happened long ago, in historical time. However, according to the mystics, creation is really something that is happening all the time. Every morning in the traditional Hebrew prayer service the following phrase is recited: "The one who renews in his goodness every day, always, the act of creation." This echoes the view that creation is not an event that occurred at some moment in past time, but rather that creation is something that is occurring at all times. The cosmic force of creation is manifesting and enlivening reality in each and every moment.

In the Kabbalah, there are actually many cosmic forces at play in this moment-to-moment process of creation. These forces are represented by the various Hebrew divine names found in the Hebrew Bible, and they also make up the constellation of what are called the *sefirot*, the divine qualities. These forces constitute both the process and the material of creation itself and ultimately are not separate from each other; rather, they reflect and express the many facets of one unified reality.

The most common divine name found in the Bible that represents these forces of creation—and the most important one in the Kabbalistic teachings and practices—is YHVH, commonly referred to as Yahweh, or the *tetragrammaton*. YHVH represents the totality of Being, including the formless inner nature of existence as well as the infinite variety of ways that the formless mystery expresses itself in the world of appearances.

If you look in an English Bible, *YHVH* is usually translated as "Lord." However, this is not a correct translation. YHVH, in fact, is not a noun at all, but rather a portmanteau, or combination, of three verbs: HVH (*is*), HYH (*was*), and YHYH (*will be*). When you combine these three verbs together you get YHVH, which is therefore best translated as: "Is-Was-Will Be," or for short, just "Being." Is-Was-Will Being is not a static entity, it is not an "it," and it is certainly not a "he." As a verb, the term is pointing to the dynamism and aliveness of Being. It is this living dynamism that permeates and constitutes everything.

YHVH, or Being, thus represents both the inner nature of creation, the spirit that animates all of reality, as well as the expression of that inner nature into form. The latter includes the manifold variety of forms that make up the created realm: the earth, the cosmos, and all the beings they contain, whether earthly or celestial. In this sense, all of reality is Divine. As it is stated in the ancient Hebrew mystical texts: "There is no place devoid of It," referring to YHVH as the spirit of all that is.

Traditionally, the YHVH is not pronounced due to its sacredness which is why it is referred to as the "ineffable name" and often written as the four Hebrew letters that constitute it: *yud* (י), *hey* (ה), *vav* (ו), and *hey* (ה). However, if one were to attempt to pronounce the name according to its basic phonetic form, it would generate the sound of a breath. To pronounce the name is to breathe. This correlation is reflected in the traditional morning prayer: "The breath of all life blesses your name."

Each of the four letters of the YHVH, as well as the upward facing point atop the first letter *yud* (י), correspond to one of the five journeys in the Path of Primordial Light, which represent the possible modes of consciousness and experience that we encounter on the spiritual path. The upward facing point on the *yud* (י) corresponds with the journey of freedom, the *yud* (י) itself with the journey of vastness, the *hey* (ה) with the journey of wholeness, the *vav* (ו) with the journey of expansion, and the last *hey* (ה) with the journey of contraction.

Thus, the YHVH as a whole encompasses all the dimensions of reality and all the journeys, from the most sublime to the most contracted. When we are stuck inside a contracted state of being, when we are identified with our personal history and lost in our thought-stories, we are dismembered from the totality of ourselves and thus YHVH (of which we are a microcosm) is also in a state of perceived fragmentation and disunity. However, when we re-member ourselves and integrate the wisdom of the five journeys into our experience and our life, then we are embodying the ancient contemplative practice of unifying the divine name. Indeed, perhaps the most central contemplative practice in all of Kabbalah is to unify this divine name of YHVH.

So, you can see now how it is that when we take a conscious breath, we are unifying the *yud hey vav hey* in our embodied consciousness. This unified condition is what I am referring to when I talk about the state of presence. Presence is the embodied experience of pure Being, of YHVH. It is the sense of Being that is dynamically and palpably present when we are in a state of union with reality and when reality is in a state of union with us.

Now we are in a position to appreciate more deeply the contemplative meaning of the five journeys. The journey of contraction is the experience of being dis-membered from Being, of being lost in thought-stories. The journey of expansion is the embodied experience of Being, of the real body, the individual letter. The journey of wholeness is the experience of the palpable substance of Being, the essential presence that animates the Presence Body, the ink that constitutes our individual letter. The journey of vastness is the experience of the spaces between the breath and between the words—it is the blank parchment, the spacious infinite source of the breath of life and of all creation.

The journey of freedom is the experience of total Being: it is the recognition that we are simultaneously an expression of all possible forms of reality, from the contracted experience of dismemberment to the vastness of space and the absence of form. It is the freedom to be everything and nothing at all, all in the same instant. It is total Being, the totality of the *yud hey vav hey* and the radical emptiness that is its ground.

In the coming chapters, we will continue to unpack these five journeys in more experiential and metaphysical detail. For now, continue to notice your experience of the breath and the spaces between them. Consider taking some time before moving on to the next chapter to contemplate how you are being impacted by these teachings thus far, and to process your experience by writing in a journal or discussing your journey with a trusted friend.

CHAPTER 6

THE LIGHT OF BEING

J ust as the breath serves as a medium through which total Being intersects with the human body, so too, YHVH reveals itself through the human body in the form of light. If the breath is an expression of the dynamic flow of the cosmic consciousness, light is what constitutes the embodied consciousness itself. This principle is reflected in this verse from Proverbs: "For the light of YHVH, the soul of the human, penetrates all the innermost parts of the belly." This verse is stating that the light of YHVH—the light of total Being, the light that permeates all of reality—is what constitutes the human soul, the human consciousness. In this sense, we are literal embodiments of YHVH, of the divine.

In particular, the verse is pointing out how this light "seeks out" or "penetrates" the inner chambers of the belly. This describes the magnetic property of the belly center of consciousness, which serves as a living well or reservoir of this cosmic light. We want to learn how to connect more fully with this indwelling presence of light in our belly so that it becomes more available to our waking consciousness. By doing so, we will also be deepening our intimacy with the primordial light of Being and more fully inhabiting our bodies as expressions of this timeless light.

In the ancient mystical teachings, the point of light in the belly corresponds with the inner subtle womb center, or what is known in Hebrew as *shechinah*, which means "indwelling presence" or just "presence." This term refers to the palpable and embodied experience of YHVH, of Being, in human form; it is the presence of YHVH in our human experience. Cultivating this indwelling presence of divine light in our belly is thus what builds up and develops our capacity for the experience of embodied presence.

This approach also corresponds with the Hebrew mystical term *tzimtzum*, which means "concentration" or "contraction" and points to the condensation of divine light within the realm of creation. We will learn more about *tzimtzum* in the next chapter, but first, let's explore this *tzimtzum* practice, which works to concentrate and distill the light of presence in our embodied experience.

Begin by finding a comfortable position, preferably sitting with the soles of your feet making contact with the floor. However, if this position is not available to you, then any comfortable position works just fine. See if you can allow your spine to be vertical and awake but not rigid, with a sense of your head reaching toward the heavens and your pelvis and feet moving toward and connecting with the earth.

Allow your eyelids to slightly close, and begin by noticing your breath as it intersects with your body. Do not alter or change your breathing at all, just allow it to be natural and flowing according to your rhythm today. In particular, notice the sensations that you experience when your breath fills your lungs and emanates a sense of fullness down into your lower belly. With the in-breath the belly rises, and with the out-breath the belly falls. See if you can sense more deeply into these belly sensations as you breathe.

Now, connect with your inner sense of touch, as if your consciousness has fingers and can touch itself from the inside out. Allow this touching or sensing capacity of your consciousness to sense into your lower belly, about two or three fingerbreadths below the navel and the same distance inward toward the spine. Allow your consciousness to really sense into the presence and inner texture of this point.

You may try gently rocking your pelvic floor and sitz bones forward and back until you feel a clearer sense of connection with your lower belly center. It may feel like an energetic clicking-in or a sense of finding a sweet spot when your system is aligned properly. If you are having trouble feeling this specific point, then just stay with the sensations of the breath filling the lower belly more generally on the in-breath.

This is a concentration practice, which means that you want to allow your presence as much as possible to focus, gather, collect, and concentrate itself in this inner center. It's as if there is a magnetic force intensifying the concentration of presence in this location of its own accord, and you are simultaneously allowing this to happen while also actively sensing into the physical sensation of this concentration in the lower belly.

As a concentration practice, the key is to notice as much as possible whenever you are distracted by thoughts, feelings, other bodily sensations, or sounds in the space and just keep gently returning to sensing into this point until your sense of connection is stabilized and not disrupted by distractions.

Continue to practice in this way on your own for a period of time. It may be helpful to set a timer so that you can really drop into the practice and not be concerned with the time. If you can do so, I also recommend that you find a few minutes to practice this at home every day for the duration of your study of this book. Between eleven to twenty-two minutes is generally a sufficient amount of time to benefit from this practice.

An important note: I recommend that you not engage in this practice for longer than twenty-two minutes at a time, or for longer than twenty-two consecutive days, unless you are an experienced practitioner or under the guidance of a qualified teacher. This practice can generate a lot of energy in the lower centers and can cause problems for some people if it is not properly worked with.

CHAPTER 7

COSMIC BIRTH

The practice of gathering and concentrating the light of Being in the belly center cultivates the direct experience of embodied presence. Over time, this practice builds a foundation for a more steady and ongoing sense of presence in the body-consciousness, which, as we will see in the coming chapters, is important for going deeper on the path. As our concentration deepens, the gathering of presence in the belly center begins to condense and distill itself into a more refined sense of the spacious light of Being. This is experienced as a sense of palpable, yet at the same time ethereal, light.

The first act of creation according to the Bible is the formation of light. In the book of Genesis, it states: "And God said, 'Let there be light,' and there was light." This original light of creation represents the primordial innermost nature of Being, the most basic ground of existence. According to the Kabbalah, in the act of creation (which as we have seen is occurring all the time), this original light goes through a progressive series of contractions and expansions as it births existence into form in each and every moment.

In this process, the infinite light of *Ein Sof,* the unknowable source of creation, contracts and condenses itself into more finite densities of light that then enables the material world as we know it to manifest and appear. This does not happen in a linear trajectory, but rather in a spiraling dynamic cycle of contractions and expansions, similar to the human process of birth. It is through the contractions and expansions of the womb that we are birthed into life. It is also similar to the process of breathing. With each in-breath and out-breath, there is contraction and expansion, a gathering of presence and its release into spaciousness.

This process of the infinite light of *Ein Sof* birthing itself into the finite forms of the material world is *tzimtzum,* a Hebrew word meaning "contraction," "concentration," or "withdrawal." This term is first found in an ancient Midrash, where it is used to describe the concentration of the divine presence into a point of light. Specifically, this point of light is found in the space between the cherubs, two angelic figurines that hovered above the ark of the covenant in the inner sanctum of Temple in Jerusalem, the most sacred site in ancient Judaism. The cherubs, one with the face of a male child and the second with the face of a female child, faced each other and hovered above the sacred chest inside the Holy of Holies. According to the ancient tradition, the infinite light of Being concentrated itself and emanated its blessings into the earthly realm of time and space through this portal.

In the Path of Primordial Light, this point of concentrated presence between the cherubs corresponds with the belly center that we have been working with in our meditation practice. I therefore call this practice the *tzimtzum* meditation, since it helps open up this corresponding anatomical portal through which the light of Being contracts or concentrates and ultimately expands, manifesting and birthing the true body. I call this true body the Presence Body.

In the Kabbalistic teachings of the sixteenth-century mystic Isaac Luria, the term *tzimtzum* takes on a different meaning than it did in the earlier texts. For Luria, it refers to the formation of a vacuous space that is generated when *Ein Sof* contracts and withdraws into itself, leaving behind a void. Then the nondimensional light of *Ein Sof* is released back into this void, manifesting the dimensional worlds. This process reflects the dynamic, creative process of contraction and expansion. It is as if *Ein Sof* takes an in-breath into itself, leaving an empty space within which it then breathes creation into being with its out-breath.

In this sense, every time we take a breath we are reenacting this primordial act of creation on the microcosmic level. When we concentrate our presence in the lower belly point, we are harnessing and vitalizing the light of creation in our individual consciousness, our individual letter of the scroll. In this manner, we begin to develop the Presence Body, which is the true human body manifesting as a living body of presence, which simultaneously embodies the paradoxical properties of both concentration and spaciousness.

This dynamic helps us appreciate more clearly the relationship between contraction and expansion. While the sensation of contraction can at times be uncomfortable and even painful, just like in the birthing process, with each contraction there is also the potential for more space to open up, for more expansion and light to be revealed. In this sense, as it is of creation and existence more broadly, contraction is a natural, organic, and even necessary part of the journey of consciousness. As we concentrate and contract our awareness and focus more intensely, this deepening of concentration in time distills itself and opens up into more spaciousness of Being, revealing more expansiveness of light.

Just like the contractions of cosmic creation or human birth serve as organic processes that open up to expansion when fully embraced, so it is with the psychodynamic, energetic, and somatic contractions that constitute the conventional experience of human perception. In this sense, the conventional state of disconnection from Being and the feeling of being imprisoned within our historically conditioned thought-stories are not problems or mistakes to be fixed, but rather are natural processes that we want to welcome, allow, appreciate, and understand. We approach it this way not only because contractions tend to dissolve and transform into expansion when we fully experience and understand them, but more importantly, because this approach to contraction is already an expression of, and in alignment with, the wisdom of true freedom.

As mentioned earlier, the statement from *The Book of Creation*—"The end is embedded in the beginning and the beginning is embedded in the end"—reflects our understanding that the journeys of contraction and freedom are completely intertwined and ultimately unified with each other. We therefore approach the experience of contraction from the perspective of the journey of freedom, which holds that there are no "right" or "wrong"—or "good" or "bad"—experiences. All value hierarchies are erased in the experiential condition of freedom.

So, whether we are rolled up in a tight ball of reactivity, neurosis, and hatred or opened up to boundless, divine love in its purity and spaciousness, all experiences are recognized as equal parts of a singular whole. Thus, Kedumah ultimately holds a radically inclusive view in which everything is recognized to be a sacred part of the ultimately unified whole, including the most mundane, ordinary, and even disturbing experiences of contraction.

This view of freedom allows us to have our experience and learn from it without giving in to the usual judgments that come with the limited perspective of the conventional mind. This radical kind of freedom is possible when we recognize that everything in our life—all of our experience—is included and nothing is rejected. Our approach to contraction is thus a practice in and of itself, one that cultivates the sense of freedom simply by embodying the attitude and truth of freedom from the get-go.

When we sense into the *tzimtzum* point we are, in a very embodied and tangible way, opening this portal of the union of infinite and finite, formlessness and form, presence and absence, contraction and expansion. And as we deepen more into this practice, the grounded sense of the Presence Body will begin to reveal itself.

CHAPTER 8

THE END IS IN THE BEGINNING

Earlier, we explored the image of a scroll as a metaphor for the spiritual journey and the transformation of our perception. We saw how in this metaphor, the blank parchment represents the primordial ground of existence, the nonconceptual source of creation. Our basic assumption is that this blank parchment—the primordial ground of creation—is limitless and all-possible. That is to say that any manifestation or configuration of forms can display themselves upon the medium of the parchment. In this sense, you can say it is infinite in its potential. This reflects the Kabbalistic principle of *Ein Sof*—literally, "no end"—which points to the endless possibilities of the primordial ground.

Thus, the blank parchment—the primordial ground—is inherently open to all possibilities. It follows then that the blank parchment, with its infinite potential, must also have the ability to express that which is limited and finite. In other words, an infinite that cannot manifest the finite would not really be much of an infinite. To be truly infinite, it must also include the finite.

Therefore, the manifestation of a finite world, of finite experience (what we call the journey of contraction, or in some teachings, the dualistic realm of limitation and separateness) also expresses the infinite's fullest potential. In a sense, the manifestation of the physical world and the human experience of contraction—what appears to be the very opposite of the vastness that characterizes the blank parchment—ultimately fulfills the very potential of creation.

This presents us with an interesting philosophical problem. While our exploration in this book is primarily experiential, and, ultimately, all the words in this book are meant to guide us into a deeper place of presence, we also want to include the possibilities of the conventional mind and its modes of understanding. So, while everything we teach points to presence and deeper experience, it must also be logically sound even as we are not using logic for its own sake, but rather to harmonize the conventional mind so it becomes more of a bridge to presence.

The philosophical problem is that logically speaking, it does not make sense that an infinite reality can manifest a truly finite form. Finitude by definition requires ontological independence from the infinite ground, one that possesses some kind of separate existence. However, all the letters and words that manifest on the parchment are inextricably united with the parchment itself. There is no way for a letter to separate itself from the scroll, just as there is no way for us to remove ourselves from the infinite nature of reality, regardless of how contracted and alienated from the source we may experience ourselves to be.

It logically follows (in the context of this metaphor and its underlying assumptions) that true finitude is an ontological impossibility. However, epistemologically speaking (that is to say when it comes to modes of knowing and perceiving), it is certainly possible and also logically sound. While we cannot separate ourselves from the primordial source and from the essential ink that inscribes all other forms of reality, we can certainly perceive ourselves to be disconnected from the totality. In fact, this is the usual way that we experience ourselves and most of us deeply believe this to be the existential truth of reality.

The medium through which the infinite potential of the blank parchment manifests its possibilities and experiences finitude is none other than the human being. The human being expresses the fulfillment of the blank parchment's limitless possibilities precisely because we experience ourselves as finite, dualistic, limited, and split off from ultimate truth—split off from our nature and the primordial ground. To truly be infinite, reality must include everything, including the experience of being alienated and disconnected from the absolute ground. So, if we did not experience ourselves as alienated then the infinite would be limited in its possibilities. Unwittingly, our contraction and suffering constitute the very fulfillment of reality's potential.

Thus, our human suffering, born out of a contracted and limited view of what we are, is not a mistake that needs to be fixed. Rather, it is part of the intelligent design of creation itself: an expression of the freedom of reality to manifest itself according to its all-possible potential. This should come as a great relief; at the very least, we can stop beating ourselves up for feeling dualistic, finite, limited, and contracted.

No contraction can ever be anything but an expression of reality itself. By allowing, welcoming, appreciating, and understanding our limited range of experience, we are already becoming intimate with the truth of reality. Orienting ourselves in this manner brings a lot more freedom and spaciousness to the journey of self-discovery. Inquiring into our experience of contraction and suffering can therefore be transformed into an intimacy with the totality from the outset of the path.

If we take this metaphysical teaching to heart, we can begin to see that it is possible to wake up to our true ontological nature in the midst of suffering, which we discover is inseparable from, and in a state of absolute unity with, the totality. Ultimately, on the Kedumah path, we go through an epistemological transformation (a transformation of our perception) to recognize what was, is, and always will be our deepest nature. You can say that it is a process whereby our epistemology is synced up with our ontology (our perception is synced up with the way things actually are), and we discover that indeed the "end is embedded in the beginning and the beginning is embedded in the end."

So, take a moment to connect with presence, with Being. First, take a full breath and as you release the breath, relax the thinking mind and drop into the space of Being in the lower belly center. After taking a few breaths in this manner, return to your normal breathing pattern and gently bring your attention to the sensations in the lower belly. If it is available to you, sense into the point of light inside the inner womb of your belly, where your presence is always-already birthing, where the light of YHVH is always-already shining.

Continue to practice in this way for several minutes, sensing into this point, allowing your consciousness to gather and concentrate itself in this magical portal of light.

CHAPTER 9

THE TREE OF KNOWLEDGE OF GOOD AND EVIL

I n chapter 8, we explored the origins of contraction from the cosmic, or macro, perspective. Now let us examine it from the personal, or micro, vantage point. How is it that we became the kinds of human beings that we are, with our limited range of perception and experience?

In Kedumah, the process of disconnection from the parchment and its infinite possibilities—of losing touch with a more expanded perception of who we are—is understood to occur in childhood. We assume that we come into this world with an open and uncluttered consciousness, an intrinsic connection to Being, and a clear and undistorted perception. And then, in the course of our development, our conceptual capacities expand along with our nervous system and structural anatomy. In this process, our physical organism and psyche develop in dynamic relationship with our early environment.

Essentially, our psychological organization, along with its sense of identity, is a product of our historical experience of being in relationship with our parents, caregivers, siblings, friends, and broader environment.

This is also reflected in the metaphor of the scroll, where our individual letter acquires meaning and is solely defined by the context of the letters around it and the words they form together. In the conventional view, a standalone letter does not express very much; it is dependent on other letters and words to fully function. Likewise, we each develop our sense of identity, value, and meaning through the narratives that we form with other individuals (the letters) and with our families, communities, traditions, country, and so on (the words and sentences). In time, we internalize these relational dynamics of our early environment, which yields a cohesive internal family system in its own right.

Thus, in this developmental process, we transition from being an open and transparent organ of raw, unfiltered perception (the blank parchment) into a more structured and circumscribed psychic phenomenon (the words and narratives). Or in other words, in the development of the psyche in childhood, our *context* eventually becomes the *subtext* of our identity narrative, or personal history. This personal history includes the internalized narratives (born out of our childhood context) that shape our individual identity narrative. Then, the psychic apparatus functions to filter the immediacy of our raw perception, inscribing our experience on our scroll in a manner that fits with the subtext of our personal history.

The subtext of our personal life is therefore constituted by the combination of conscious and unconscious psychic structures that determine our experience and define who we are—or, more accurately, who we take ourselves to be. The process of moving from contraction to expansion thus will ultimately require us to reveal the unconscious subtext that forms the background parchment of our conscious lives. It will require us to learn how to unpack the multiple layers of meaning that are hidden within the words and letters of our personal scroll.

This whole process of psychic development is reflected in the Garden of Eden story found in the book of Genesis. In chapter 2, the text describes how God instructs Adam not to eat of the Tree of the Knowledge of Good and Evil. But in chapter 3, when Eve recalls the instructions in her interaction with the serpent, she actually changes certain details of the instructions. Eve's modifications point to this process of psychic development, resulting in a perceptual disconnect from our divine source.

Let us compare the two formulations of this injunction:

Genesis 2:16–17	Genesis 3:2
"You must not eat from the Tree of the Knowledge of Good and Evil, for when you eat from it you will certainly die."	"God did say, 'You must not eat fruit from the tree that is in the middle of the garden, and you must not touch it, lest you will die.'"

Eve makes several changes when she relates God's instructions to the serpent. The first change is that she adds the word "fruit," which is not included in the original version. Secondly, she changes the wording to "the tree that is in the middle of the garden" leaving out the phrase "Tree of the Knowledge of Good and Evil." Thirdly, she adds a brand new requirement that "you must not touch [the fruit]." Lastly, she changes the wording from "you will certainly die" to "lest you will die."

These subtle changes in Eve's phraseology suggest a psychological process at play in her communication with the serpent. On one hand, her modifications seek to downplay the severity of the prohibition while on the other, they expand its range. For our purposes, the most significant changes are the extension of the prohibition to include touching the tree and the downgrading to the milder punishment of "lest you will die." Eve's modifications suggest that she is already contemplating eating from the tree, so much so that she feels the need to put up additional boundaries ("you must not touch it") around the core of the prohibition. Such additional boundaries would only be necessary if there was some sense that the actual prohibition was close to being violated. Furthermore, by downplaying the severity of the punishment, Eve indicates her unconscious interest to partake of the tree, which she ultimately acts upon.

Eve's inner conflict around eating of the tree represents the classic human struggle between our instinctual drives and our spiritual impulse toward truth. In human development, this conflict becomes the key fulcrum in our perceptual shift from rootedness in Being (our original condition in the Garden of Eden and in early childhood) to contraction (our condition after eating of the tree and in the developmental process as children).

So, we can now appreciate how the individual and personal human experience of contraction is a natural and organic expression of the psyche's developmental process. This process is also reflected beautifully in the biblical text when deciphered through a more mystical, psychodynamic lens. In this reading, Eve and Adam represent the archetypes of our human psychological condition. Consequently, the day to day struggle with one's conflicting inner parts is not a mistake nor an error that we need to try to reject; instead, it is a valid experience.

In the next chapter, we will continue exploring the origins of human contraction. As you contemplate these teachings, continue to drop into your embodied felt-sense experience in your lower belly, sensing into the light of Being, the infinite light of your embodied soul.

CHAPTER 10

THE MOTHER
OF ALL LIFE

We have been exploring in the past few chapters the origins of contraction, and how it is that as human beings we tend to perceive reality through a narrow, limited range of experience. In particular, we have seen how the Garden of Eden story reflects the process of human development from a more open, expanded, mode of perceiving, into a more closed, contracted, state of awareness.

Our understanding of this process deepens as the narrative unfolds in chapter 3 in the book of Genesis. After Adam and Eve eat of the Tree of the Knowledge of Good and Evil, the verse states that their "eyes were opened, and they realized that they were naked." But they were already naked prior to realizing it, so what is this shift in their perception?

If you think about it, nakedness only makes sense if we are being seen by someone outside of ourselves. That is, we experience ourselves as naked because we are perceived to be naked. So, nakedness really describes a certain kind of perception that only exists when another person perceives us this way. If nobody, including our own self-consciousness, is there to see us, then we would not consider ourselves to be naked.

This suggests that after eating of the tree, Adam and Eve shifted to a mode of experience whereby there was a distinction between observer and observed, between subject and object. Another way to say it is that their state shifted from a nondual mode of experience to a dualistic mode of experience, one in which they experienced themselves as separate from the object of their perception.

In the mystical traditions, *nondual realization* refers to a way of perceiving in which there is no separation between subject and object. The one seeing and that which is being seen are experienced as one unified reality. The usual mode of perception is called *dualistic*, one in which we experience ourselves (the subject) as seeing something outside of ourselves, something separate (the object). Thus, the eating of the tree and the opening of the eyes brings about a radical shift in the human being's experience. It represents the shift from our original nondual perception (where there is a unified field of experience) to a dualistic mode of perception, one which is marked by a subject-object divide.

The original condition of human consciousness that existed prior to this shift correlates in human development with our infancy and experience of early childhood, in which our consciousness is quite open and expanded, raw in the now of our experience. In contrast, our conditioned and contracted mode of experience correlates with our conventional sense of reality that develops in early childhood and crystallizes in early adulthood. The Garden of Eden narrative thus articulates one ancient mythological account of the origins of the human condition of contraction.

Before Adam and Eve eat of the tree, the text calls Eve by the Hebrew name *Isha*, which literally means "woman." It is not until after they eat of the tree that she is given the name *Chavah*, which is the name typically translated into English as "Eve." The text explains that the reason her name is changed to Chavah is because "she would become the mother of all the living." But what does the word *Chavah* actually mean?

While the name Chavah is linguistically similar to the Hebrew word *chaya*, which means "living" or "living being," it is a distinct word with different root-letters and has no clear etymological relationship with *chaya*. Etymologically, it is more similar to another biblical word that means "to speak" or "to express," as in a verse from Psalms: "Night to night bespeaks wisdom." In this verse, the verb "bespeaks" is *yichaveh*, which comes from the same root as *chava*. This word is also similar to the Aramaic word *chivyah*, which means "serpent." That Isha is renamed Chavah, a word that philologically relates to the words for "speaking" and "serpent," suggests a lot about the psychological dynamics at play in this narrative and the archetypal roots of our human situation.

As we saw in chapter 9, Eve was already experiencing some kind of inner conflict about the commandment to not eat from the tree. Her inner conflict and ambivalence about the restriction expressed itself in her conversation with the serpent, where she hedges the original formulation of the prohibition. But is her conversation with the serpent a real interaction with an ontologically separate being (the serpent), or is it simply an external projection of her own inner psychic dynamic?

By giving her the name Chavah, which can be interpreted to mean "speaking-serpent," the Torah is suggesting that the conversation that Eve is having with the serpent is really an externalized projection of her own inner process. It is also significant that she is given this name because she "would become the mother of all the living." That is, she represents the mythological prototype for the human being, characterized both by psychological structures and impulses (which are oftentimes in conflict with each other), as well as by the ability of each part of our psyches to interact and "speak" with the others.

So, we see that Chavah represents the conflicted internal system of the developing human psyche, mythically portrayed in this ancient biblical narrative. In Kedumah, our psychodynamic issues and conflicts are thus appreciated as one of the chief expressions of a dualistic and contracted view of ourselves and reality. It follows that at the initial stages of the spiritual journey, working with our psychodynamic issues becomes a crucial doorway into more expanded modes of being. By understanding our psychic structures and their limiting influence on our perception, these structures can then unwind and be seen through, ultimately returning our consciousness to its original pristine condition of unobstructed perception.

By concentrating presence in our lower belly center, the *tzimtzum* practice helps establish the capacity to stay more grounded and present in our embodied consciousness, in the here and now of our experience. It helps shift the compulsion of our mind away from its identifications with the conflicting forces of our psyche and into the here-now reality of presence. In particular, along with the other practices throughout this book, it begins to reconnect us to our original mode of perception, that which we embodied prior to eating of the

Tree of the Knowledge of Good and Evil; that is, before adopting a dualistic, contracted view of reality.

Through accessing this embodied nondual mode of consciousness, we can approach our psychic structures—our self-concepts, internalized beliefs, self-images, identifications—with more space and dis-identification, which in time permits us to understand them and experience the contractions they hold more completely. This process then transforms and opens up our experience into the journey of expansion.

Before you move on to the next chapter, take some time to practice the *tzimtzum* meditation (described above in chapter 6) and if you can, journal about your experience and your process and/or discuss them with a trusted friend. In particular, reflect on how the practices and teachings are impacting you personally. Note your insights and any inner revelations you may be experiencing as well as any reactions or difficulties that may be arising.

⟨ CHAPTER 11 ⟩

AWAKENING THE PRESENCE BODY

The journey of contraction describes conventional perception—it's the limited and imprisoned way we usually perceive and know ourselves, others, and reality. All wisdom traditions in one way or another are responding to this state of contraction, offering mythologies that explain the origins of our suffering, as well as various technologies that prescribe how to find freedom from this situation.

One major way that we maintain this contracted state of mind is through a deep identification with our physical body as a separate entity, isolated from other bodies. This view is so fundamental to the organization of our psyche and our sense of self that it's rarely challenged. It's such a given that even when we experience expanded states of being—such as oneness, unity, nonduality, etc.—the snapback into a more familiar sense of encapsulation within our skin is usually pretty quick. There are many subtle dimensions to this instinctual snapback into the boundaries of our physicality, but at its core is the entrenched belief that we are defined and confined by our physical bodies. Inherent to this belief is the basic assumption that our existence is first, dependent on the survival of our physical organism and second, limited to the dimensions of the physical body in time and space.

Over the past several chapters, we have been exploring how the Garden of Eden narrative outlines the origins of our human condition of contraction. In particular, we saw how Chavah, as the "mother of all life," represents the prototype of our human psyche with its inner sense of conflict. As the narrative unfolds in the book of Genesis, the focus shifts from the development of the conflicted human psyche to the development of this deep attachment to the physical body as an encapsulated organism separate from other bodies. This is the billiard-ball model of reality, where we perceive ourselves to be separate balls of matter that are basically bumping into each other and other objects.

In the verse immediately following the one in which Eve is named Chavah, the text states: "And YHVH God made garments of skin for Adam and his wife and he clothed them." The Hebrew wisdom masters point out that the Hebrew word for "skin" (עוֹר) is almost identical to the word for "light" (אוֹר). Both words have nearly identical modern pronunciations (*ohr*) and only differ by one letter. If you spell the word with the letter *ayin*, it means "skin"; if you spell it with *aleph*, it means "light."

This points to how our true body is constituted by light, and it is only through the perceptual shift into duality that occurs after eating of the tree that we perceive ourselves to be encapsulated by skin. So, the transformation is from bodies of light to bodies of skin. Thus, one consequence of eating of the Tree of the Knowledge of

Good and Evil is that there is a narrowing of our view whereby we cease experiencing our bodies as constituted by the essential light of presence and instead perceive our bodies as encapsulated by skin. That is, we shift from nondual perception to a dualistic experience of separateness.

The spiritual journey back to the primordial ground of our consciousness and ultimately into freedom thus entails a reintegration of our original body of light and its nondual mode of perception into our everyday experience. The journey calls us to dissolve the conceptual overlay of our skin as constituting a separating boundary and calls us to return to the primordial Eden, our original state of being: the body of light or the Presence Body.

The way we accomplish this return back to our true body of nondual presence is through cultivating a more direct intimacy with our embodied experience. After the realization of their nakedness and the fashioning of garments (both of which reflect the shift into dualistic, contracted modes of perceiving), the text states that "Adam knew his wife, Eve." The word "knew," from the Hebrew *da'at*, clearly does not refer to intellectual knowing but rather to intimate knowing; that is, physical unification, the union of flesh. The text clarifies this by stating: "And they became one flesh."

So, the Torah here is showing us how we can move from a dualistic, contracted mode of experience back to our original nondual body of expansive light. This is accomplished through cultivating and expressing our inner connection and union with our own bodies, our physicality. Certainly, physical intimacy with another person is a very powerful way to experience a sense of greater union with reality. Interpenetrating with another body is a great way to overcome and dissolve our perceived boundaries of skin.

However, on the mystical level, another person is not required for the fulfillment of this process. Since Adam and Eve represent the archetypal masculine and feminine principles of consciousness, these two facets are intrinsic to each one of us. In this sense, Adam "knowing" Eve and "becoming one flesh" points to an internal potential that we each have to unify our own dismembered consciousness through remembering ourselves, through embracing and actualizing a deeper intimacy with our own bodies, our own sensual flesh.

So, let's explore three related practices that use the wisdom of inner touch to shift into a more immediate and intimate experience with our embodied potential, which can help us re-establish our conscious connection to our inner body of light. Like the practice of taking a conscious breath, the following technique can be utilized at any time, regardless of where you are, what position you are in, or what you are doing. This practice, along with the next two in chapters 12 and 13, are really just different variations of the same basic practice, building upon the *tzimtzum* meditation by helping to expand the light of the soul from the lower belly center into and through the entire physical body.

In this practice, we will sense into the inner sensation of our hands from the inside out. You can try this right now. Wherever you find yourself right now, and whatever you are doing, just sense into the inner light of your hands through inner touch. Take a few moments to really feel into the texture, tone, and viscosity of the hands and fingers. As you allow your consciousness to intensify its inner sensing, you may start to feel a buzzing or vibration in your hands, which may be very subtle or may be quite pronounced. If you allow this ethereal buzzing or vibration to fully display itself, it will naturally begin to expand to include the entire body. See what it's like to feel into this for a moment.

In the next chapter, we will build upon this technique and learn a more expanded version of this practice that applies this same method to the entire physical body. So, before you move onto the next chapter, I suggest that you continue to play with sensing your hands throughout your day or night, pausing every now and then to sense into the living presence of your hands, noticing your embodied experience and your state of consciousness.

CHAPTER 12

PURIFICATION
OF THE LIMBS

The practice of sensing into the hands is an easy way to connect to the Presence Body since it links into the inner channel of presence that extends from the lower belly center out through the arms and legs. The following practice builds upon that practice and is derived from a Kabbalistic text that describes a mystical technique called "purification of the limbs."

This practice trains the limbs of the body to become vehicles for the experience of embodied presence. Unlike body-scanning meditations such as mindfulness-based stress reduction (MBSR) and other Buddhist-inspired mindfulness practices that work from the outside in, in this practice, we want to allow the self-sensing presence of the inner body to awaken and come alive from the inside out. Instead of focusing on being aware of bodily sensations, we want to activate the sensate body to become aware of itself through intimate touch.

So, begin by finding a comfortable position, preferably sitting with your feet on the floor. However, if that is not available to you, then any comfortable position works just fine. Allow your spine to be vertical yet not rigid, natural, and at ease, with a sense of your head reaching toward heaven and your feet grounded on earth. Begin by allowing your consciousness to sense itself as the feet. Sense into your toes—more through allowing your embodied presence to sense itself *as* the toes.

What's it like to sense into the bones of the toes, and the tissues that connect them? What's the space and volume like of each toe when you sense into them? Expand your sensing now into the rest of the foot, allowing your consciousness to sense into the space that fills each of the feet. Simultaneously sense now into the bones of the feet and toes along with the space and volume of the feet and toes.

Breathing freely and fully, allow your breath also to participate in the sensing. Add now your ankles, sensing into the space, bones, cartilage, connective tissues, ligaments, and tendons. Continue to allow the sensing presence to fill the space of each of the feet from the toes up to the ankles. Now add the lower legs, allowing presence to fill, sense, and feel through the legs from the inside out. Sense the two bones in the lower legs, the tibia and fibula. Now, see if you can drop into and sense the interosseous membrane, the space in between the two bones. Notice the three-dimensionality of each of the two legs—the volume and the space. Continue to allow a state of no-mind and raw, immediate sense perception. Add now the knees, sensing and touching into the intricacy of the anatomy in each of the knees. Now add the upper legs. Sense into the powerful muscles—the hamstrings and the quadriceps. Also, include the femur bone itself, really touching into it by allowing your sensing presence to touch itself as the femur.

Add now both hips. Continue to allow your breathing to naturally be full—filling both legs from the bottom of the feet and the toes all the way up to the hips. Notice the pelvis itself, the pelvic bowl. Don't notice with the mind, but rather notice through the direct intimacy of touch. Touch into the pelvic bowl with its organs of vitality and delicacy—the genitals and the perineum. Sense into the lower belly, into the womb.

Now add the hands, starting with the fingertips. Allow the presence to sense itself in each of the fingers, sensing into the bones, connective tissues, and muscles. Can you sense each of the joints in the fingers? Notice the volume and the three-dimensionality of the hands. Add now the wrists, lower arms, and forearms—each of which holds two bones, the radius and ulna. Sense into these two bones as well as into the space between them.

Allow your breath to continue to be full and easy, naturally filling the spaces of the body. Allow your presence to continue to sense itself as the body from the inside out. Add now your elbows and your upper arms. Sense into the humerus bone along with the muscles of the biceps and the triceps. What's it like to just be in the raw immediacy of contact without separation between the observer and that which is observed? Feel the pure, raw, sensate perception.

Now add the shoulders and allow both arms from the fingertips up to the shoulders to be alive with a sensing presence along with both legs from the feet up to the hips. So now, we have both legs and both arms sensing themselves—present, awake, alive. Now, sense into the lower belly and diaphragm, and up through the whole torso and into the chest. Notice the dimensionality, the full cylinder of the torso filling with self-sensing presence.

Allow presence to sense itself in the neck, the throat, the cervical spine, all the way up into the face and the cranium. Notice the dimensionality of the cranium along with the intricate bones and muscles that comprise the facial structures. Sense front to back, side to side. Sense the volume of the cranial space.

Notice what it's like to touch into the top of the head and the space above the top of the head. Notice the column of space as it opens up and connects us from our core all the way through the top of the head. Allow the self-sensing presence to continue to be uninterrupted through both arms and legs.

Now, just notice what it's like to hear the various sounds in the environment around you. But don't hear them with your ordinary ears, listen to them from the sensing body of presence. And now, just notice what it's like to read these words not with your ordinary eyes but from the presence of the body itself. Allow the sensing Presence Body to look at the letters and words. Slowly look around at the space around you and see what it's like to perceive your environment—to see and to hear—from the perspective of the self-sensing Presence Body.

While this marks the end of the formal guided practice, the practice can continue throughout your day or night. As the self-sensing presence of the body awakens, your center of perception shifts more fully into the immediacy of what you are, into the nonconceptual nature of your living body of presence.

CHAPTER 13

THE PRESENCE VEHICLE

The third technique in this series of inner sensing practices is to sense the totality of the body from the inside out in a single instant. You can try this right now: See what it's like to sense, all at once, into your entire body from the inside out. Take a moment to explore dropping into this more global sensing practice. You can play with this practice anytime, wherever you may find yourself and in the midst of whatever you are doing in everyday life. Just bring your attention to your entire body-soul from the inside out: sensing, feeling.

In this practice, we are approaching the inner body of light directly through a more global sense of the body-soul. It is as if in each instant, we are sensing into our entire body-consciousness. You might find this practice to be accessible and natural, and it will bring an immediate shift to your consciousness. If this is the case, you will start to feel the sense of a palpable, subtly vibrating presence taking the place of your usual sense of your body. If, on the other hand, this practice does not come easily to you, then spend more time with the first two sensing practices in chapters 11 and 12. Over time, you will find it easier to drop into sensing your global inner body more at will.

Once you feel that you have a sense of the subtly pulsating presence of your body, then you can add looking and listening. With this additional component, the flesh of the Presence Body is what is now seeing and hearing all the sense perceptions in your field. When we gaze at our environment through the living body of presence, we see that it is possible to be grounded and centered in ourselves as an individual letter in our own right while at the same time experiencing ourselves as inseparable from—and an integral expression of—the whole. We find that one of the chief features of the Presence Body is that it is both concentrated and dense while at the same time spacious and expanded.

The Presence Body practices that we have been exploring generate the inner vehicle through which we will ultimately be able to perceive all of reality as an expression of Being all the time, even in the hustle and bustle of everyday life. As you learn to settle more into the immediacy of presence, even the usual distracting sights and sounds of a busy city, for example, are no longer problems but fascinating wonders to behold. The potential for our flesh and bones to become the eyes and ears of nondual perception is also reflected in this verse from the book of Job: "From my flesh, I shall see God."

So, we see that the process of returning to our original condition of nondual perception requires us to re-member and reclaim our primordial body of light. In order to understand this more deeply, it will be helpful to return to our earlier exploration of the phenomenon of contraction. Usually, we understand contraction to refer to something that is constricted and closed in on itself. But the term can also signify a certain kind of concentration. It can be the concentration of energy, presence, or awareness.

As we learned in chapter 6, the Kabbalists refer to this multivalent principle of contraction with the term *tzimtzum*. *Tzimtzum* refers both to concentration as well as the process of creating an empty space, an inward expansion of energy through the action of cosmic "withdrawal." The word thus embodies a core paradox on the path of awakening that we may be beginning to see with the *tzimtzum* practice: The more that we concentrate our presence and awareness into a singular point, the more spaciousness and expansiveness arises.

The ancient Hebrew wisdom masters teach that the divine presence, the *Shechinah*, "contracted" or "concentrated" herself (the term used there is *tzimtzum*) into a tiny point in the space between the cherubs that hovered above the ark of the covenant. Thus, we see that the cherubs are intimately connected to the divine presence; in fact, they are the primary vehicle through which the presence is able to manifest into the physical realm of time and space.

Let's explore this more deeply. The ancient prophet Ezekiel, whose mystical vision of a *merkavah* serves as one of the foundational texts of the Kabbalah, attains prophecy through gazing into the river called *Kevar* (כבר), a word meaning "always-already," which points to the mystical understanding that presence is always-already present in the eternal here and now. *Kevar* also shares the same three root letters as both *keruv* (כרב), meaning "cherub," and *merkavah* (רכב), meaning "chariot" or "vehicle." The cherubs feature as an important motif in the Kabbalistic teachings on the *merkavah* based on the first chapter of Ezekiel, a text revered in the Kabbalah as containing the keys to attaining prophecy and mystical enlightenment.

So, we see that the divine presence is inextricably connected to the *keruvim* (plural of *keruv*), the *merkavah*, and the river *Kevar*, which is the always-already lens of presence through which the prophetic vision is attained. In some sense, these terms all point to different kinds of conduits or vehicles for the presence to manifest within the created realm of time and space. Throughout the Hebrew Bible, this same three-letter root then appears again in the form of the "blessing," the *beracha* (ברכ), that is passed down to the *bechor*, the "firstborn" (בכר), as a lineage transmission from generation to generation.

The transmission of this constellation of inner principles embodied through the terms "always-already-presence-vehicle-blessing-firstborn-cherubs"—which are all intimately connected through the shared three-letter root—contains the experiential keys that can unlock our original human condition, the one that we possessed in the Garden of Eden prior to the eating of the Tree of the Knowledge of Good and Evil. This presence-blessing, then, encodes the secret formula to embody the presence in the concentrated form that is required for the transformation of contraction into expansion. It is the means through which we develop the embodied presence necessary to free our perception so we can begin to see that our true body is not contained by skin but rather consists of boundless light.

Let us now bring this back to the Garden of Eden narrative. When we last left Adam and Eve (see chapter 11) they had perceived that they were naked and their bodies of light were replaced with garments of skin. Immediately following this, the text states that Adam and Eve were expelled from the garden and God "placed cherubs (*keruvim*) at the east of the garden." As we now know, the *keruvim* represent the vehicle for the concentrated manifestation of the presence, sharing the same root letters as *merkavah*, *kevar*, *beracha*, and *bechor*. But what does it mean that they were placed at the east of the garden?

"Placed" in Hebrew is *vayashkein*, which shares the same three root letters as the word *shechinah*, the classical term that represents the embodied divine presence. Furthermore, the term translated here as "east" in Hebrew is *kedem*, literally "primordial" or "ancient," which shares the same root as the word *kedumah*, the primordial ground of reality, and the name of this teaching.

The terms *kedem* and *kedumah* point to the original primordial condition, the blank parchment of the scroll. The terms *vayashkein* and *shechinah* point to the manifestation of this primordial nature into the created realm of time and space, the embodiment of the formless into form—the ink, letters, and words of the scroll. The *keruvim* and the *merkavah* thus represent the potential of our consciousness to become mystical vehicles of perception that seamlessly integrate the physical realm of form with the invisible realms of formlessness.

Thus, the integration of the blank parchment and the embodied individual letter—our innermost nature and our mundane human experience—is the ultimate fulfillment of "the end is embedded in the beginning and the beginning is embedded in the end." It is the gateway back to our original primordial nature, the nonconceptual source that is always-already present in the here and now of our ordinary experience.

So, take a moment to sense into the totality of your body-soul, as well as into that point of light between your cherubs, your *keruvim*. See what it's like to feel into your individual *merkavah*, your living body of presence that is always-already shining with the lineage of your soul, with the eternal birthright of the primordial light of boundless freedom.

CHAPTER 14

THE TREE OF LIFE

I n the last chapter, we saw how we become a *merkavah*—a presence vehicle—when we integrate the body of light, when we become a Presence Body. However, what makes a vehicle a vehicle
is its capacity to move. In the case of the *merkavah*, its particular
function is to travel through inner space, through the hidden dimensions of consciousness. It is the vehicle of presence through which we
traverse the five journeys, from contraction all the way to freedom.

In the ancient Hebrew mystical tradition, there are two major
categories of wisdom teachings. The first is called *ma'aseh bereishit*
(the "workings of creation") and the second is *ma'aseh merkavah* (the
"working of the chariot" or "workings of the vehicle"). The foundational teachings that we have been learning thus far derive from
the *ma'aseh bereishit* school, the creation teachings. The creation
teachings provide us with a clear understanding of the view of the
path and they show us how to awaken our consciousness to presence.

The vehicle teachings, on the other hand, show us how to travel
through the inner space of the five journeys *with* presence and

ultimately *as* presence. As we approach the halfway point of this book, we are now beginning our transition from the creation teachings into the vehicle teachings.

In the Kabbalah, the term *merkavah* refers to an inner vehicle of consciousness that is used to journey through the many hidden dimensions of reality. It is also a code term for the constellation of the *sefirot*, the divine qualities that make up the Tree of Life, which is the central map of consciousness in the Jewish mystical tradition.

Traditionally, the Tree of Life depicts the essential ingredients that make up the totality of creation, which as we have seen is total Being or YHVH. These essential ingredients are the *sefirot*, which derive from a Hebrew word that means something like "luminous." I therefore refer to the *sefirot* as the "lights of Being," as they represent the different qualities, aspects, or colors of pure divine light that constitute both the hidden cosmic realms as well as the earthly domain of human experience.

When the formless, colorless light of *Ein Sof* (the endless mystery) re-enters the vacuous space of the void that is formed during the primordial process of *tzimtzum*, the light is refracted through the prism of the primordial Torah into ten distinct colors, which are the ten *sefirot* of the Tree of Life. These lights include qualities such as love, compassion, strength, wisdom, understanding, and so on.

Since the human being is a microcosm of the cosmic totality, the Tree of Life is also a map of the human body and consciousness. Each *sefirah* (which is the singular for *sefirot*) therefore correlates with a different anatomical region of the body as well as with a particular aspect or quality of presence that can be experienced through the prism of human consciousness. The function of the *sefirot* is to provide the infinite mystery with a functional and relational body of perception and expression. They are the infinite's eyes, ears, and limbs, which allow the infinite to experience and live a finite human life.

When we awaken our consciousness and embody presence, we are helping to fulfill the purpose of creation by essentially transforming our bodies into vehicles for the totality to consciously experience itself as an individual human. The Presence Body is thus the interface through which the finite and the infinite meet.

The most important principle to understand here is that all human experiences—including our painful, contracted experiences of suffering—are necessarily expressions of these *sefirot*, these pure lights of Being that constitute everything in reality. If our experience is marked by a certain expansion and clarity of light, then we are experiencing the lights of Being more clearly and without obstruction. If, however, our experience is marked by contraction and suffering, then that is an indication that one of the pure lights of Being is obstructed or distorted in our consciousness.

Anytime we experience an inner conflict, it means that one of the lights of our Presence Body—our individual Tree of Life—is cut off from our awareness or dimmed of its brightness. For example, if we notice that we are experiencing inner conflict or ambivalence about a relationship, then we are cut off from one or more of these lights of Being. It may be that we are cut off from the quality of strength, so we are unable to separate from the relationship. Or, we may be cut off from the quality of merging love, so we are unable to fully commit to being vulnerable and intimate. Instead of just making a clear choice to either be fully present in the relationship or to fully leave it, we feel stuck and trapped, typically feeling as though we are a victim or perhaps overtly blaming the other person for our inner turmoil.

However, once we have connected enough with our own capacity for embodied presence, then we can work more effectively with our contractions. By effectively, I mean we can work with our contractions in a manner that does not bypass them but rather digests and distills them into essential nutrients so that our soul can more fully metabolize these pure lights of Being in our consciousness and into our life.

Basically, the way it works is that all of our contractions manifest on some level through our embodied experience. This means that all of our unresolved psychodynamic and emotional conflicts, issues, difficulties, anxieties, wounds, fears, and traumas all have somatic presentations and representations. Our bodies reflect both the cosmic and individual totalities: this is the principle of the "end is embedded in the beginning and the beginning is embedded in the end."

Therefore, as we become more connected to our embodied experience through the inner sensing practices that we have been learning, we are both pushing up to the surface more of the content of our unconscious and undigested psychic material, and in the process, we also have more of an opportunity to metabolize our contractions more consciously, with the light of presence serving as the alchemical agent of transformation.

In the previous example of someone suffering from inner conflict about a relationship, this practice would entail staying as embodied and present as possible with the intense sensations of discomfort and claustrophobia that arise when we consider fully committing to the relationship, or to the intense sensations of fear and anxiety that come up when we consider fully leaving it.

When we are able to stay embodied and fully present to our suffering sensations without repressing them or acting them out by attacking or blaming ourselves or others, then the contraction transforms into one of these luminous lights of Being. Specifically, it transforms into the very quality of light that our soul needs to fully meet the particular life situation that we are struggling with.

So, continue to play with one or all of the practices that we have learned so far: Taking a conscious breath, noticing the spaces between the breaths, sensing into the vibrations of the sounds of the words that you hear and the spaces between them, sensing into the lower belly point, sensing into the hands, sensing into the arms and legs, and sensing into the totality of the body all in a single instant. And then, from whatever presence you are feeling, practice perceiving—looking and listening—from that presence.

In the coming chapters, we will be learning how to use the fruits of these practices to stay more present when difficult experiences arise. With a bit of guidance and practice, it is totally possible for our suffering to transform into freedom.

CHAPTER 15

GOING DOWN
TO GO UP

The journey from contraction to expansion is about waking up to presence and working with our suffering in a way that transforms it into spaciousness and freedom. There are two interrelated approaches to this process, both of which are based on the Hebrew mystical principle that everything in creation contains an outer light and an inner light. This dialectical relationship is also reflected in the Kabbalistic teaching that YHVH "surrounds all the worlds" and also "fills all the worlds." We also see this concept come up in the teaching that there are two categories of spiritual awakening: "awakening from above" or just "waking up" and "awakening from below" or "waking down."

We can access the light of Being or YHVH, which is the state of expansion, from these two vantage points: without or within, above or below—from outside of our particular experience of suffering or from deep within it. The practices that we have been exploring thus far really work both sides of this process. Taking a conscious breath and dropping into presence by releasing the thinking mind; bringing awareness to the in-between spaces; noticing the vibration of letters, words, and the spaces between them; and reading this book from a place of presence all bring us more in touch with the light surrounding—the light above—our experience.

That is, these practices attune our consciousness to the presence that permeates the atmosphere around us so that we can be more open to its light. This is what we mean by waking up. The *tzimtzum* practice and the other inner sensing practices develop our capacity to stay with our experience long enough that the light within (or below) can reveal itself to us from within our experience. This is what we mean by waking down.

The first category of practices works more predominantly with expanding our awareness to reveal the space all around us, and the second category works more predominantly to concentrate and distill the material of our consciousness to reveal the space within us. Both of these categories of practice help shift our experience from contraction into expansion, but they do so from different angles, each employing different technologies. These two approaches also resonate beautifully with recent quantum science discoveries demonstrating that vast space both surrounds and fills all matter.

There is also an important distinction between these two approaches in terms of their function on the path of awakening. The first approach, that of waking up, has the benefit of more quickly opening up our awareness to expansiveness. However, if we are only aware of the nondual space that surrounds our experience of suffering and we don't appreciate the nondual space that is within our experience of suffering, then we will be one step removed from our totality. This approach of awakening from above is really just the first step on the spiritual journey. We need to first wake up to the fact that there is more to reality than what our thinking mind has us believe. And we need to recognize that our experience of suffering is like a cropped photograph that appears to be all dark gray, but when we zoom out, we see that the dark gray is really just a cloud surrounded by a vast, open sky. This zooming out is what we mean by waking up, and it can happen in all kinds of ways: through meditation, prayer, sacred study, or ritual; through the transmission of nondual states from a teacher; through making love; or even through shock, such as the death of a loved one or a traumatic accident.

But when viewed from the perspective of the awakened state, it is clear that none of these practices or events produce the primordial ground of our being (as our innermost nature is always-already existent), but they can help to foster a more conducive atmosphere for waking up to occur. This is what we are doing in this book. Ultimately, however, as we will see later on, waking up happens through grace. When waking up does happen, we realize that we are not limited by the content of our experience, but that who we are includes the infinite space surrounding our experience of suffering. This is generally the first step on the path.

The second approach of transforming contraction to expansion works more with the material of our experience as portals into expansion. In this waking down approach, we learn how to stay present and awake as much as possible while turning toward our painful experiences of contraction and suffering. We do this primarily through the body since it is closest to us and the most accessible portal to all of our unconscious psychic material. The *tzimtzum* meditation and the other inner sensing practices all cultivate this capacity to wake down into our experience more fully. In the Hebrew mystical tradition, this approach is called *yeridah k'tzorech aliyah*, which means "going down for the sake of going up." That is, by going more deeply into our experience of suffering, we open up the inner light of spaciousness and love within it, which then expands into and integrates with the surrounding space and light.

Ultimately, regardless of which direction we approach it from, the evolutionary process of awakening will compel us toward the unification of the inner and outer lights, of the above and the below. YHVH is ultimately one unified reality. The view that these lights are separate from each other is the result of dualistic thinking and is ultimately a perceptual error that is corrected on the path. All of the practices that we have been exploring ultimately seek to merge above and below, unifying the *yud hey vav hey*. For example, we include the spaces between the breaths as well as the breath itself, and when we cultivate the Presence Body, we also add looking at and listening to the spaces around us. Ultimately, these practices reveal to us that the inner and outer, the above and below, that which surrounds and that which fills is all one unified truth.

This realization of the integrative union between the outer and inner light is the hallmark realization of the journey of wholeness. Wholeness is marked by the healing of the split between inner and outer, between above and below. It is the integration of our essential soul-substance of the ink; it's the metabolism of our personal history and all its content of experience with the open sky that surrounds us. It's deeper than expansion alone because it does not orient itself in contrast to contraction but rather includes both contraction and expansion as two sides of the same phenomenon.

The reason why we emphasize waking down in Kedumah is because it is necessary for the journey of wholeness to open up and work its magic on us. It is through the journey of wholeness that the lights of Being, the *sefirot* of the Tree of Life, establish themselves in us and act through us. At the heart of every contraction is the vast light of Being, of deep and profound peace, and this light is the portal to the divine qualities or cosmic branches of our individual tree of life.

In the coming chapters, we will further clarify both the process of waking up and waking down because they are both necessary and integral for the journey of wholeness to open up. In particular, we want to learn how to wake down in order to wake up: that is, how to approach our experience of contraction in a manner that will open it up into expansion and beyond—to wholeness, vastness, and freedom.

As we are now at the halfway mark of this book, it is a good time to reflect on your personal experience of these teachings and to journal about your experience and process thus far. How are these teachings affecting you? What are you learning about yourself as you explore the practices? Is anything different about your experience and your consciousness since you started reading this book? If so, what is different? What questions do you still have? What do you hope to learn with the rest of the book?

CHAPTER 16

EROTIC AWAKENING

One simple practice that you can do anytime and anywhere to help deepen your experience of presence is to become aware of consciousness itself. Let's try this right now. Take a moment to look around at your environment and notice the visuals that you see and the sounds that you hear. All of these sense-perceptions represent the current content of your experience. Now, also become aware of the perceiver, the consciousness that is perceiving all of these images and sounds. Notice what you experience right now when you become aware of the experiencing consciousness itself. You may notice a palpable yet subtle pulsing of presence, of consciousness, at your core. This living consciousness is presence.

In this practice, we are adding another dimension to our repertoire of techniques to help us shift our consciousness out of its habitual mode of identifying with the content of our experience into sensing more directly the experiencing consciousness itself, which is the Presence Body.

In chapter 11, we learned about the principle of *da'at*, which means "knowledge," and how true knowledge is one that is embodied and in direct union with the object of our knowing. We saw how this was reflected in the biblical narrative of Adam "knowing" his wife Eve, and how this culminates in them becoming one flesh. This principle points to how in deep intimacy, the knower and the known can become one unified whole, one truth. When the knower and the known become one, we are abiding in the nondual state of being where there is no longer a subject-object divide. This is the quintessential state of spiritual awakening or enlightenment recognized by many mystical traditions.

The principle of *da'at*, of intimate knowing, takes on even greater significance in the Kabbalah, where it represents the most unique of all the lights of Being, of all the *sefirot* in the Tree of Life. It is unique because it is the only *sefirah* that is usually not counted among the ten standard *sefirot*, and it is also usually not included in the diagram of the Tree of Life. This is because according to the Kabbalists, *da'at* is not exactly a divine quality in the same way the others are. It is really the hidden unifying property that operates through all the qualities, the essential glue that unifies the entire Tree of Life. According to the texts, the state of mystical union (called *devekut* in Hebrew, which literally means "cleaving to"), is achieved through the realization of the potential of *da'at*, of embodied nondual intimacy with our experience in the here and now.

Waking up to presence is thus really about waking up our innate potential for *da'at*—true nondual knowing—to freely operate as a unifying force through our embodied consciousness. According to the Kabbalah, when we are born, the quality of *da'at* is not yet activated in our organism. It is in a state of latency, meaning it is dormant deep within our nervous system, and it only first comes on board at the age of sexual maturity: twelve for a girl and thirteen for a boy. With the activation of sexual energy, which is the essence of *da'at*, we develop the capacity for creating life through embodied union, through intimacy of flesh. So, we see that *da'at* is essentially our sexual energy, which is the energy of creation itself, that force within us that is propelled toward intimacy, union, and the formation of new life.

This erotic energy expresses itself through our entire being in different ways. One of the ways the kabbalists map out human consciousness is through the three primary centers of the Tree of Life: The belly center, the heart center, and the head center. The belly center, which also includes the genitals and reproductive organs, correlates with the *sefirot* known in Hebrew as *netzach, hod, yesod,* and *malchut*. The heart center correlates with *chesed, gevurah,* and *tiferet*; and the head center correlates with *keter, chochmah,* and *binah.*

So, the principle of intimate knowing, *da'at*, expresses itself through the belly center as the grounded, steady, inner-sensing and inner-touching presence in the belly and entire body. The first half of this book emphasizes the belly center since it establishes the foundation of the Presence Body as well as the *merkavah*, the presence vehicle. Through the heart center, this life force expresses itself as desire and longing. In this sense, all of our desire is driven on a deeper level by a pull toward intimacy and union with reality. Even material and carnal desires are animated at their core by a drive toward the union of our consciousness with the totality. The trick in working with desire is to feel it as much as possible on this deeper level, to allow the erotic, raw energy of desire to fill our entire body-soul and to make inner contact with whatever the truth of our experience is in the moment.

In this sense, truth itself—the truth of our experience, the truth of reality—becomes the deepest object of our heart's desire. So, it's important that we don't repress our erotic energy; we want to allow it to flow and to express itself fully. At the same time, we don't want to act the energy out in harmful ways. Rather, we want to fully feel it through our cells, to allow its intensity to build and ultimately nourish and transform us from the inside out.

In the ancient Hebrew tradition, truth is YHVH itself; it is the inner nature of reality, the spirit that animates everything. In the daily prayer service, we recite the formula: "YHVH our God, is Truth." And in the Talmud, it states that "the seal of YHVH is Truth." So, you can say that to learn how to wake down, how to turn the *merkavah* on to journey into the depths of our being, we need to set the navigational system of our heart to be guided by a desire to know the truth. This is why in the Kabbalah, the principle of truth is correlated with the heart center of consciousness. Specifically, we need the heart to want to seek the truth for its own sake, not to achieve any particular result or to avoid any particular pain. This orienting principle of the heart, to seek truth for its own sake, is necessary for the *merkavah* to penetrate our deep inner space.

Through the head center, true knowledge paradoxically reveals itself to us through adopting an inner posture of not-knowing, of being open to a radically fresh and new revelation in the moment without overlaying our past experience. This understanding is exemplified in the statement of the Hasidic master Zvi Hirsch of Zidichov, that the fulfillment of *da'at* is when one "knows that they do not know." Embodying true *da'at*—true knowing—requires that we accept that we do not know anything and are open to being surprised by what reveals itself to us.

So, we need to get turned on to the erotic force of intimate knowing in our soul so that we can turn toward our experience with an embodied presence, an attitude of heartfelt interest and desire to uncover the truth for its own sake, and the openness of not-knowing in our head center. We want to learn how to approach our experience just as we would want to be approached by a lover. What kind of presence from our lover do we respond to? What do we relax and open up to? What do we trust?

Most of us respond to a steady presence that offers genuine love, interest, and curiosity about us as well as an openness to the moment without overlaying past experience or assumptions. With the embodiment of these three inner centers, our inner vehicle of consciousness—our *merkavah*—will be prepared to meet our experience in a manner that will invite and encourage presence to reveal its deeper secrets to us.

So, between now and the next chapter, continue to play with the practice of shifting your awareness from the content of your experience to the experiencing consciousness itself and notice how it affects your experience of presence. Pause for a few seconds during your day and bring your awareness to the one who is perceiving, the one who is experiencing. Adding this dimension of awareness to daily life as well as to all the other practices that we have been learning can help integrate more deeply the nondual wisdom of *da'at*.

CHAPTER 17

NOW THE TRUTH

Perhaps the most central contemplative practice in all of traditional Judaism is inquiry into the truth of the Torah. This practice is called *drash*, which means to "seek out" or to "inquire." Traditionally, this does not just entail studying the Bible but includes the deep contemplation of the oral teachings, the Talmud, and its many layers of commentaries. The key orienting principle in this practice is called *Torah Lishmah*, which means to study Torah for its own sake, for the pure love of the truth, for the love of total Being. For this reason, the phrase *Torah Lishmah* is also understood by the sages to mean "Torah for the sake of the Name," that is, of the divine name.

On the mystical level, both the written and oral dimensions of Torah are literal expressions of divinity. As such, the contemplative study of Torah is a way to seek out and know God, to become intimate with the divine. In the Zohar, the practice of contemplative Torah study is described in explicitly erotic terms. The process entails removing the garments of Torah through deconstructing the narrative layer of meaning in order to penetrate into her body and ultimately into her secret hidden depths, which results in the mystical experience of union with divinity and reality. This is achieved by applying the principle of intimate knowing on the path of inquiry.

In Kedumah, we apply the same approach of inquiry to our personal experience in the here and now. This is because according to the tradition, the human being is the embodiment of a Torah scroll; we too are living incarnations of the totality. So, the traditional practice of erotic inquiry into the truth of the Torah is here applied as an intimate and embodied engagement with the truth of our own inner experience, with the totality of our personal scroll.

In this practice, we are activating and bringing into alignment the three centers of consciousness—the head, heart, and belly—in our individual, as well as cosmic, tree of life. This begins to bring the central channel of the Tree of Life into harmony and alignment, which is necessary for the *merkavah* to guide us into the deeper mysteries of Being. You can say that the *merkavah* is the Presence Body turned on to inquire into the truth of our experience in the here and now.

Orienting our consciousness to seek out and inquire into the truth as a path of spiritual awakening has its roots in the mystical meaning of the Hebrew word for truth itself, which is *emet* (אמת). The word has a unique construction in Hebrew since the first letter of the word—*alef* (א)—is the very first letter of the alphabet, the last letter—*tav* (ת)—is the very last letter of the alphabet, and the middle letter—*mem* (מ)—is the very middle letter of the alphabet.

According to the most ancient Kabbalistic text, *The Book of Creation*, all of creation is an expression of the Hebrew letters and numbers. The three letters *alef, mem,* and *tav* thus symbolize or point to the totality of the Hebrew alphabet, which is the totality of creation. It is the totality of the cosmos— the divine itself. When we say "God" in this tradition, we mean the very Being of creation in its totality, the one dynamic Is-Was-Will Beingness that we are all part of. It is not only that God is in us; we are also in God.

According to the ancient texts, the unique construction of the word *emet* also reflects the dimension of time. *Alef* is past, *mem* is present, and *tav* is future. If, as we previously learned, YHVH (Is-Was-Will Be) is truth, then we can begin to outline the nature of this equation more precisely. *Alef* corresponds to "was," *mem* to "is," and *tav* to "will be." It thus makes sense how truth—*emet*—is Is-Was-Will Be, total Being.

Let's look at this more deeply. If *alef* is past, *mem* is present, and *tav* is future, then *emet* holds an even deeper secret in terms of our orientation to the three centers. And this secret can be discovered through a deeper exploration of the letter *mem. Mem* is significant in the ancient Hebrew tradition in several ways. First, let's take a brief look at numerology. Much of the Western tradition of sacred numerology comes from a numeric system called *gematria,* the system of sacred correspondences between the numbers and letters in the ancient Hebrew tradition. In this tradition, every letter in the Hebrew alphabet is assigned a numerical value, and *mem's* numerical value is forty. The number forty appears many times in the Torah: Noah's flood lasted forty days, Moses spent forty days on the mountain waiting to receive the Torah, for forty years the Israelites wandered in the desert—the list goes on. The question is, why forty? The number forty, *mem,* has to do with the potential for transformation that is present in every moment. If we are able to immerse ourselves completely in the moment (or perhaps we should call it the *mement*) then transformation is guaranteed.

For example, *mem*, or forty, is the required volume of water in a kosher *mikvah*. A *mikvah* is an ancient ritual bath that continues to be used today by traditional observers of Judaism as a means of purification of the body-soul. There are very strict ancient laws that determine what constitutes a kosher *mikvah*—that is, one that is fit for ritual use. One of the requirements is that it contain forty *se'ah* (an ancient measure of volume) of water. Forty is therefore not only transformative in the realm of time but also in the realm of space. In this example, a body of living water constitutes the transformative space.

Interestingly enough, the great medieval sage Maimonides, who was not a Kabbalist but instead posited an Aristotelian metaphysics, has a fascinating comment in his magnum opus, a code of law called the Mishneh Torah. In the section that discusses the laws of a *mikvah*, he states that if you do not have an actual *mikvah* available, entering into "waters of *da'at*" allows one to experience the same process of purification and transformation of consciousness.

In this book, we are learning how to embody these "waters of *da'at*"—the forty *se'ah* of the *mikvah*—in our being, immediately and directly. These are the waters of nondual intimacy with our experience in the here and now, which is the essence of the journey of expansion. The letter *mem*, the number forty, and the present moment are the truth. The heart of the truth, the *mem*, which is at the center of *emet*, is the now. For us to enter into the waters of *da'at*, of true knowing, our heart needs to engage our experience in the now as fully and completely as possible. This is the deeper meaning of the ancient Hebrew teaching that "the truth will set you free." By dropping into the heart of truth—the present moment—we find the freedom of expansion.

So, take a full conscious breath, and as you release the breath, release and relax your thinking mind, dropping into the waters of true knowing, the waters of the now. As you breathe, include in your awareness the experiencing consciousness itself, the one who is breathing and perceiving everything.

Notice what it's like to engage this practice now, at this point in your study of this book. Notice if it feels easier to drop into a space of presence now than it did when you first tried this practice back in chapter 1. As you move on to the coming chapters, continue to play with the practices of conscious breathing as well as with the other inner sensing practices, becoming aware not just of the content and the vibrations they carry, but also of the consciousness itself, of that which is experiencing the content. And as much as possible, use the wisdom of these practices to drop more deeply into the now.

---— ◆ CHAPTER 18 ◆ ———

THE PRIMORDIAL
SCREAM

The process of *yeridah ketzorech aliya*—of "going down in order to go up" or "waking down in order to wake up"—begins with the very raw acknowledgment of the fragility of our situation, of our vulnerability and the primal nature of our helplessness as human beings. The prototype for this process of waking down in order to wake up is described in the book of Exodus with the enslavement of the children of Israel in Egypt. The Hebrew word for Israel is *Yisrael* (literally, "one who wrestles with God"), and Egypt is *Mitzrayim* (literally, the "narrow" or "contracted" places).

So, on a deeper level, the narrative of the Israelites being enslaved in Egypt points to the archetypal human journey of suffering, one that pertains to all of us who wrestle with God regardless of our tradition or culture. It speaks to all of us who experience a disconnect from the boundless love and goodness of reality, all of us who experience ourselves as stuck and imprisoned in a contracted state of being.

According to the ancient Hebrew tradition, the number fifty represents the principle of completion and wholeness. The ancient texts state that at the time of their enslavement, the Israelites had reached the forty-ninth level of disconnection from their source in the Tree of Life. That level marks an almost complete dismemberment from Being, from the totality. They were almost at the point of no return. Yet, it was precisely in these darkest depths of despair, precisely at the point of almost complete alienation from God that the Torah states that children of Israel cried out for help. The text states, *venitzak el YHVH*, which means "And we cried out to YHVH." The text continues: "And YHVH heard our voice . . . and YHVH brought us out of contraction with an outstretched arm and a mighty hand."

Once they had reached a point of near total desperation, when they had hit rock bottom, a primal call for help arose from their depths. This moment represents a turning point on the spiritual journey and in the human journey in general. To what degree are we able to acknowledge the depths of our vulnerability as human beings? All of us have suffered losses, wounds, pains, tragedies, and injustices of all kinds. How many times have our hearts been broken, have our spirits been crushed, have our bodies been shattered? How many times have we witnessed the fragility of human life? To allow in the raw vulnerability of the truth that life is precarious marks the beginning of the transformative process of waking down, of transforming our contraction into expansion.

When we feel into this very delicate internal space, we realize that to become free from our inner prison we need an awakening from above. At this juncture, we accept that all of our ordinary resources and capacities cannot heal us, cannot undo what has been done, cannot fix what has been broken. At this point, we recognize that without some kind of magic we have no hope for recovery. It's only when we touch into this most vulnerable place of need inside our being that the alchemical shift of consciousness is possible. This step begins with a release of energy that comes out of the belly and body as a primordial scream, a calling forth from our depths. This primordial scream, this call for help, is really a call for freedom, for redemption. It is a call for healing, for magic. This is the meaning of the verse in Psalms that states: "From contraction I cry out to you, God. Answer me, God, from expansion."

According to the tradition, the most effective prayers—the ones that are most readily answered—are those that emanate from a place of pain and suffering. With the primordial scream practice, we are not reciting liturgical formulas but instead are crying out from the depths of our being, from the rawness of our human vulnerability. The sound that needs to be released is the primordial and primal call of the cosmic totality itself, calling out to itself for healing. With this practice, we are building upon our earlier practices of belly concentration, breath, and inner sensing to tap into and make contact with that place in our being where the primordial and the primal interpenetrate, where "the end is embedded in the beginning and the beginning is embedded in the end." In this place, our scream becomes the deep calling unto and upon the vastness of space; it is the inner light calling upon the outer light. It is the totality calling itself unto itself. This is a call for magic, for grace, for an awakening from above through an awakening of below.

So, let's explore this practice. Begin by connecting with your embodied presence. You can do this by sensing into your hands or through sensing into the global sense of your entire body. Also include an awareness of that which is sensing, of the experiencing consciousness itself. Once you feel some sense of connection to your embodied presence, notice if there are any contractions or wounds that show up in your body at this time. It could be a more nonspecific global sense of contraction or disturbance in your system or there may be a specific wound that you feel in a particular location or region of your body.

The first step is to locate the contraction in your body. So, take a moment to see what shows up right now in your embodied experience. See if there is a particular contraction or disturbing experience that wants to be worked with. Once you find it, feel into it and sense its texture, tone, and visceral quality. See if you can sense into the very heart of it; see if you can feel into its very center.

At this point, there are two different variations you can take. If you are in a space where you can scream as loudly as you want without disturbing anyone (perhaps a soundproof room or an isolated area of nature) then the first variation is for you. If you do not have that privacy, the next paragraph will describe how you can modify the practice. For the first variation, from the innermost center of the contraction, extend your arms and hands up and out to the sides. With your palms open and arms reaching diagonally upward making a "v" shape, slightly lift your chin up toward the heavens. Harnessing all of the primal energy in your body from the pain of your contraction and with your mouth opened wide, unleash a wild scream out to the universe. Feel it through your entire body-soul, allowing your body to express the sound as fully as your voice does. Feel the vibrations of your scream stretch out to the far reaches of the cosmos, feel it ripple through the entire universe. Make the sound as loudly, powerfully, and viscerally as you can. It can be done repeatedly several times until you feel some kind of inner shift or a sense of completion.

The second variation of the practice is called the "silent scream." It contains all the same elements as the first version, the only difference being that the actual sound is not released. All of the visceral body sensations are fully felt and expressed along with the movements of your mouth, throat, torso, diaphragm, and belly as if you were releasing the sound. The energy is released even though the actual voice is not released with sound. The benefit of the silent scream is that it can be done anywhere and at any time. So, if you find yourself in an emotionally or energetically difficult and painful contraction, you can take a pause, go to a separate room where you can close the door, and do this practice.

So, between now and the next lesson takes some time to experiment with the primordial scream or the silent scream. Whenever you feel a contracted experience, first connect to presence, then viscerally locate and feel into the contraction in your body. Sense into its center as much as possible and notice what happens in your experience and your consciousness when you allow yourself to call out to the universe for grace, for magic.

CHAPTER 19

THE MOUTH
THAT SPEAKS

Waking down into the raw and vulnerable experience of contraction is necessary for us to begin to re-member ourselves and our true inner nature, to reintegrate the lights of Being into our day-to-day experience of life, and to re-establish our roots in the cosmic Tree of Life. The primordial scream is one expression of this deep vulnerability, which is the feeling of being disconnected from our true nature, from the Tree of Life, from the totality of who and what we are. At the same time, embodying the power of the scream and allowing ourselves to become vehicles for its primal expression helps us begin reclaiming our essential voice and plugging it back into its power-source in our Presence Body and in the cosmic Tree of Life.

So, the process of waking down begins with the primordial scream, which is a release of many layers of accumulated tensions and energetic patterns in the body-soul. This release not only invites in the loving expansive light of YHVH, which is the awakening from above, but it also opens up more space for us to begin to turn more fully toward the somatic, energetic, and psychic dimensions of our contractions themselves. These dimensions can then provide us with a more lasting transformation of our psyche, of the very wiring of our nervous system.

With the reclaiming of our inner voice through the primordial scream, the process of waking down can now progress to include the power of our speech as a way to further facilitate the transformation of contraction into expansion. This is reflected in the ritualized telling of the story of the exodus from Egypt that is performed at the Passover *seder*, the ceremonial feast on the first night of this ancient festival. The main text that is read at the *seder* is called the *haggadah*, the "telling," the main section of which is known as *magid*, which also means the "telling." The mystical sages also point out that the Hebrew word for Passover, *Pesach*, can be read as two words combined—*pe* and *sach*. *Pe* means "mouth" and *sach* means "speaks." The whole holiday thus has to do with the mouth that speaks. So, you see there is a very ancient understanding of the power of speech on the journey of waking down into contraction as a way to wake up into expansion.

According to the ancient Kabbalists, the exile into Egypt (*Mitzrayim*) was an exile of *da'at*. *Da'at* as we have seen is intimate knowing, the state of embodied nondual presence. So, *Mitzrayim*—literally translated as "contraction"—represents a state of disconnection from the immediacy of our experience in the here and now. Since *da'at* is the underlying property of all of the lights of Being—of all the qualities and colors of creation—then if it is in exile it makes sense that we would not have experiential access to any of the lights.

The movement from contraction to expansion requires the actualization and the reintegration of *da'at* into our felt-sense awareness. This requires the intimate union of flesh and perception that is accomplished through the practice of embodied sensing that we have been exploring throughout this book. It is also aligned with the living dynamism and eros of the heart and the engaged wakefulness and openness of the mind.

According to the Zohar, the exile of *Mitzrayim*, the contraction, was not only an exile of *da'at* but also an exile of *dibur*—"speech"— which means that reclaiming our embodied experience of presence along with freeing our speech is itself the way out of Egypt, the way out of enslavement to our contractions. Thus, sensing into our embodied experience in the here and now while speaking out loud the truth of our experience is the magical cocktail for reintegrating these two essential elements of our nature that have been lost in the experience of contraction. By reintegrating these lost aspects of our consciousness, we also reclaim the state of expansion.

This deep relationship between *da'at* and speech is also reflected in the Kabbalah, where the quality or *sefirah* of *da'at* is correlated with the throat center of consciousness in the Tree of Life. So, there is an inner channel of presence that moves from our embodied experience of presence through our throat and expresses itself through us as true speech. This permits us to establish our expansiveness in a more enduring manner, just as the verse in Psalms states: "True speech endures forever."

In particular, the ancient Kabbalistic texts describe an inner channel that threads the heart to two organs of our being: the tongue and the genitals. Erotically, this makes sense given the centrality of the mouth and the genitals in the expression of eros, which is fundamentally grounded in the heart's desire and engagement with the intimacy of the moment. Eros can be expressed both with another person or on one's own in the form of intimacy with one's own life force. Both the tongue and the genitals perform the particular function of expressing our heart and sharing it with the world and with others.

So, when the tongue speaks the truth, both of which are grounded in the center of the heart, then the mouth becomes an organ of creation. In the book of Genesis, it states: "And God said 'let there be light,' and there was light." So, the act of creation occurs through divine speech. We see here the potential for human beings to be God incarnate, to create light and blessing—as well as, God forbid, destruction and harm—through the expression of our tongue, which is connected in this invisible channel with the heart. You can now see the deep relationship between speech, truth, contraction, expansion, and the power of creation.

So, we are seeing how speaking of the truth is a method in and of itself for spiritual awakening, which is why sharing our process with a trusted friend and speaking to our own personal experience of contraction can be a powerful way to move from contraction to expansion. This is why one of the main practices that we do in Kedumah is to share embodied presence and speak about the truth of our experience with one another.

When we integrate the three orienting postures—grounded presence in the belly, love of truth for its own sake in the heart, and the openness of not-knowing in the head—and include the expressive potential of the tongue and the genitals, then we have the workings of the *merkavah*. In Kedumah, the *merkavah* is the essential form our consciousness takes when it becomes an instrument for the spontaneous expression of *drash*, which we learned is the practice of inquiry. And in its optimized form, inquiry is the immediate, open, engaged, grounded, and spontaneous inquiry into the here and now.

But, this is only possible when the very substance of our body-soul—our living consciousness—manifests as the mystical vehicle of the *merkavah*. For this to happen, the three centers of the central channel of the Tree of Life (the head, heart, and belly) need to be integrated and activated along with the expressive potential of the genitals and the tongue. When the Presence Body engages as the *merkavah*, then speech becomes not just a mechanism of transforming expansion into contraction but also an integrative mechanism of unifying the inner and outer lights. And further, it is a means of re-membering the cut-off lights of Being, which is the essence of the journey of wholeness.

So, let's explore this together. This practice builds upon the previous chapter's exploration of the primordial scream. Begin by taking a moment to connect with your embodied experience. Sense into your hands or into your entire inner body, or take a few conscious breaths. Then just notice what you are experiencing right now. See if there is any disturbance or contraction that is present in your field of consciousness or in your body.

From this place of embodied intimacy with your experience, see what it's like to really step into the felt sense of the contraction. And then, from this place, practice speaking out loud your experience to the benevolent spirit that is animating the universe. It may be helpful to place an empty chair across from you so that you can imagine the empty chair inhabited by God.

Similar to the primordial scream, in this practice we are allowing the individual consciousness to commune with the cosmic consciousness, the inner light to commune with the outer light. The practice is to voice your experience with words, even if it feels weird or contrived. If the truth of your experience is that you feel uncomfortable with the practice, then that is what you express with speech to the living Being, the totality. Set aside some time to experiment with this practice, and notice what you experience in your consciousness and in your life.

CHAPTER 20

SPEAK TO YOUR CHILDREN

I n the last chapter, we explored the metaphysical and experiential power of speech and how it is rooted in the cosmic act of creation. Since the human being is a microcosm of the totality, the divine speech that created the world is available to us through human speech. In particular, when our tongue is synced up with our inner central channel of creation (including the heart and genitals), then our speech becomes a vehicle for presence to transmit its blessings into the world of creation. It also becomes a mechanism for us to deepen into our process of waking down into the inner light of our experience, which opens up more of the spaciousness of expansion.

If you are a person with speech or hearing loss, then know that whenever I use the term "speech" or discuss the power of words, on the deepest level, I am talking about the inner channel of presence that expresses itself through whatever forms of communication we have available to us. So, however you are able to communicate works just as well as speech with respect to the inner journey.

As discussed in chapter 19, the ancient festival of Passover reflects this process. On the mystical level, it celebrates the potential for each and every one of us to experience inner freedom from our own psychic contractions, right here and now. At the *seder*, the following phrase is recited: "Every single year we are required to see ourselves as if we ourselves are being freed from *Mitzrayim*, from contraction." The guiding principle here is that mystically speaking, the redemption from Egypt was not a historical event but rather serves as a contemplative symbol about the potential of our consciousness to free itself right here and now from the contracted modes that confine us day to day.

The function of the ritual feast of the *seder* is therefore to facilitate this experiential process of moving from contraction to expansion, from enslavement to freedom. This is accomplished primarily through speech, through telling the story of the exodus. The requirement to tell the story of the movement from contraction to expansion on Passover (*Pesach*, deconstructed to mean, "the mouth that speaks"), is rooted in a verse from the Torah that states: "And you shall tell your children." The mystical sages point out that the Hebrew word for "and you shall tell," *vehigadeta*, is understood through its Aramaic translation to mean to "draw down" or to "transmit." So, the function of speech in this sense is to transmit or draw down the light of presence and the experiential knowledge that the tale of freedom carries.

Specifically, speaking the words and telling the ancestral story reminds us that while it is painful to feel stuck in dark places of contraction, there is a loving light of presence that will respond to us if we call to it. The mystical sages emphasize that the chief energetic transmission of the first night of Passover is that of unconditional love. And the way we invoke that boundless love is through transmission: telling the tale, speaking about our experience of contraction and our past experiences of moving from contraction into expansion.

Interestingly, the verse specifically states that we are required to transmit this experiential understanding to our children, which is why if you have ever attended a traditional *seder*, you may have noticed that much of it is designed to keep the children engaged and participating. However, on the contemplative level, the commandment to "speak to our children" is really calling us to engage and transmit to our *inner* children, to all of the young and wounded parts of our psyche that are in need of love, care, and attention. These inner children are all of our contractions, and, in one way or another, have their origins in the early childhood experiences of disconnection and dismemberment from Being and from the Tree of Life. Therefore, what our contractions need most of all is to re-connect to Being, to re-member presence.

This healing process ultimately can only be accomplished through our own loving engagement with these child parts from the perspective of our adult presence, from a state of *da'at* or true embodied knowing. Specifically, they need the grounded presence of our belly, the care and interest of our heart, and the openness of our mind. And these parts need us to speak to them with words that are grounded in the experience of and connection with presence, which carries with it the transmission of the unconditional love and light of expansion.

When we hear words that are grounded in presence and divine love we can feel the clarity and unconditional benevolence that they carry. The loving light that permeates these words is experienced as a pure, clear, golden light that surrounds and fills us with the most delicate pure love. In the presence of this loving light, we feel in the depths of our being that everything is okay, that we are okay, that we are held and cherished. We feel its clarity, spaciousness, softness, and care for us personally as well as the radical way that it is untethered from all of our personal history. This loving light does not relate to us based on our past. Rather, there is a radical freshness that is steady, sure, and unmoved by all the surface garments of the world. The light of divine love contains no motivation to change or fix our experience, yet magically it's in the presence of this unconditional love that we are transformed and healed.

So, waking down in order to wake up is exemplified on the night of Passover by an act of grace, an awakening of unconditional love from above that reaches down with "a mighty hand and an outstretched arm" and lifts us up and out of our hole of despair, out of our prison of contraction and suffering. In this experience, we see clearly that there is a loving light that surrounds us and a loving light that fills us and that we are fundamentally infused with this inner-outer light. It's like we wake up and realize that, lo and behold, in the presence of this light there's all kinds of space to move about that we didn't even know existed.

The practice we explored in chapter 19 of speaking to the benevolent spirit that animates all of reality from the place of contraction is thus only one side of the process. The other side is to speak to our contractions, to our children, from the place of the loving light that is animating all of reality. The light that surrounds speaks to the light that fills. What is it like to turn toward our contracted experience from the perspective of the true parent, from our seat in presence? This presence mother or father is our own Presence Body, itself an intimate expression of the loving light of divinity. What is it like to speak and commune with these difficult and painful places inside of us from God's seat, so to speak?

So, begin by taking a moment to connect with your embodied experience. Sense into your hands or into your entire inner body, or take a few conscious breaths. Then just notice what you are experiencing right now. Now, consciously take the seat of the boundless light of expansion, the loving divine light—sit in God's seat. It may be helpful to do this with an actual empty chair across from you, so you are speaking to your "children" that occupy the chair across from you as you inhabit God's seat.

This alone will immediately shift your consciousness. Then, from this place, practice speaking out loud to your contractions, to the parts of you that are suffering, that are in pain or feel stuck and imprisoned. From this place, speak to your children. In this practice, we are allowing the cosmic consciousness to commune with the individual consciousness, the outer light to commune with the inner light. So, set aside some time to experiment and explore this practice before you move onto the next chapter. Notice what you experience and how it affects your state of consciousness.

CHAPTER 21

THE INSIDE IS LIKE THE OUTSIDE

O ver the past few chapters we have been exploring speaking to God from the seat of our contractions as well as speaking to our contractions from the seat of God. These practices allow our words to flow freely and spontaneously, going with whatever comes out in the present moment. You can also experiment with having a more dynamic exchange between these two aspects of your being—between the seat of God and that of your inner child-part. These practices can help heal our wounds and also start to bridge the gap between our inner and outer dimensions of experience, between our inner and outer lights. They can also help deepen our trust in the perfection and benevolence of creation itself, as it states in the biblical verse: "I trust because I speak."

According to the Talmud, the mark of a complete human being is someone who is *tocho kevaro*, which is an Aramaic phrase that means someone whose "inside is like their outside." So, human completion or wholeness is characterized by a unification of the inner and the outer, a union of the light that fills and the light that surrounds. In this sense, everything that we have been practicing thus far has been guiding us toward a deeper understanding of this principle and a deeper experience of our potential for wholeness, for union with the totality of Being.

If the journey of expansion is marked by the discovery of the inner and outer dimensions of presence, the journey of wholeness is marked by the union of the inner and the outer into an integrated, coherent, and unified human being. This journey, which is an integration of the journeys of contraction and expansion, reveals a more coherent and cohesive Presence Body, one that is constituted by the essential substance of creation itself, the ink that animates all the letters and words of the scroll. The ink is, you can say, the essential substance through which the infinite and the finite meet. It is the interface between the individual letters and the blank parchment.

The complete human being is thus simultaneously both completely physical and completely spiritual; she is divinity enfleshed and physicality ensouled not as separate realities, but as two sides of the same unified truth. At this point of intersection, where the inner and the outer meet, a new human being is born—a new individual presence is birthed. Perfectly positioned at the nexus between heaven and earth, this new kind of human being is uniquely situated to fulfill the purpose of creation whereby the infinite reveals itself as the finite.

Transparent to the light from above and endowed with the earthly capacities to navigate and function within the realms of time and space, this complete human being becomes a lens through which the infinite gazes into the finite and the finite gazes into the infinite. It is the vehicle through which the infinite wakes down into human experience and the finite wakes up to its infinite nature.

In this sense, this integrated inner-outer Presence Body is the earthly embodiment of the Kedumah principle, which as we learned in the very first chapter, is the cosmic interface between the infinite and the finite. The mark of wholeness is thus the ability to act and interact on the earthly, or horizontal, plane of reality in a manner that is aligned with—and an expression of—the vertical truth of infinity. Thus, the realization of wholeness is really the meeting of the vertical and the horizontal dimensions of reality in the individual human consciousness.

However, true wholeness cannot be limited to an individual realization or experience. The ink is the essential substance of all the letters on the scroll. It is the unifying force that animates the collective soul, the communal organism of presence. This is reflected in the ancient Kabbalistic teaching that there is one unified cosmic soul, a primordial soul, of which we are all individual sparks, each of us a chip off the old block, as it were. Insofar as we are dismembered from the one cosmic soul, the human collective is in a state of brokenness.

The task of repairing and reconstituting the unified human soul is what the Kabbalists call *tikkun*, meaning "repair." As such, true wholeness must also reveal and express itself through the re-memberment, the putting back together, of the collective human Presence Body. This is accomplished primarily through relating and living with each other from a state of embodied presence that expresses the wisdom of our individual tree of life, with all of its lights of Being.

So, we see that the journey of wholeness really calls us to fill out our presence into the horizontal dimension of human expression, into the sphere of the collective and communal dimension of relationships and interactive living. In this process, we build what the Hebrew mystics called a *dirah batachtonim*, a "dwelling place below" for the cosmic totality. In this way, we fulfill the collective human mission of completing the infinite loop of creation—we thread the beginning into the end and the end into the beginning.

One of the primary ways we embody and express our presence with each other is through our speech, through generating a creative field that is charged and primed with the light of Being. As we have seen, speech is even more primordial than even light and breath since it is the very source of creation, the source of light and breath. This is why working with speech as a practice is so powerful as an integrative, unifying path to wholeness.

In the past few chapters we have been exploring various practices that utilize the power of speech to transform our consciousness and deepen our experience of presence. Now let's introduce a further extension of these practices that utilizes speech to deepen our capacity for the horizontal filling out of our collective Presence Body, of our universal soul.

As mentioned in an earlier chapter, the central contemplative practice in traditional Judaism is studying Torah for its own sake. Traditionally, this is performed with a study partner, called in Aramaic a *chavruta*. Deep inquiry into the truth of the Torah is thus engaged in the context of relationship. This partner practice of inquiry is a very active and dynamic dialectic between the two, involving an interactive exchange of ideas and perspectives that brings the two partners closer to the truth. Closer, in fact, than they would be if each were only inquiring on their own. This potential is based on an ancient Hebrew teaching that states that whenever two people exchange words of truth, the divine presence immediately dwells between them.

To engage this practice, find a spiritual friend, an inquiry partner. It does not have to be someone you know well, it can even be someone you meet through any spiritually oriented community that you may be connected to. The practice is to explore what it's like to interact, relate, and exchange words while staying connected to your presence, to your truth. You can talk about anything at all; you can share whatever your experience is in the moment, discuss some issue you are working with or something real about your process, or relate something going on in your life that is affecting you. In this practice, it's not about the content of your words, it's about the presence that you are transmitting *through* your words. This is an exercise in training your consciousness to be able to speak words with others from a place of deep connection to yourself, to your presence.

Begin the exercise by sensing into your embodied experience and as much as possible, sensing your presence. And then as you interact, focus about 70 percent of your attention on your own inner sensing practice while you speak and listen your partner. The other 30 percent of your attention can be on the content of the words and the other sense-perceptions in the environment. Anytime you notice that your speech is disconnected from your embodied presence, just take a pause to sense into your inner body. Then, speak as slowly as you need to so that you stay connected to your Presence Body and your inner channel of intimate knowing.

Take some time to explore this partner exercise. This practice works to deepen both our personal experience of wholeness as well as to heal our collective body of presence, bringing the one cosmic soul closer to a state of *tikkun*, of repair.

CHAPTER 22

LISTEN UP

We have been exploring speech as a spiritual practice, one that can be applied both in one's individual, personal inquiry as well as relationally with others. Chapter 21 specifically explored the art of speaking to another person while staying in connection with our embodied presence. We are practicing this with the goal to do it all the time, even with people who are not oriented to presence. The rubber meets the road on the spiritual journey when we attempt to authentically express ourselves in all of our relationships as well as in all of our mundane daily activities.

Speech provides us with a way to unpack and deepen into our own experience and at the same time, it also deepens our connection to others. However, in the partner practice (and in relationships more generally), there is another side of the equation: the ability to listen to others from a place of presence. Ideally, when we listen to another person, we are also embodying the core principles of the *merkavah*: steady, grounded, embodied presence in the belly and body; interest and curiosity of the heart; and an openness and not-knowing of the mind.

Ultimately, we want to be able to deeply listen not just to other's voices (or any form of communication) but also to their inner voice, to the deeper places within them that want to be heard and seen and known. We want to listen to the presence that their words are carrying. At some point in the development of the partner practice, we realize that it is not actually the case that two separate individuals are speaking and listening to each other. We recognize directly that we are all unique cells of one cosmic body, of one unified living Being. We realize that the inner and outer lights are really one unified light; that all of reality, including all people, are constituted by the essential light of presence.

This is a core realization on the spiritual path: the discovery of the interconnectedness and oneness of all beings and all reality. This realization's intimate relationship to listening is reflected in an ancient Hebrew prayer called the *Shema*, meaning "listen." This prayer, which comes from a verse in the Hebrew Bible, is arguably the most important and central of all prayers in Judaism and is traditionally recited every morning upon rising, every night upon going to sleep, and at the moment of death.

The words of the prayer are: *Shema Yisrael Adonai Eloheinu Adonai Echad.*

The first word, *shema*, means "hear" or "listen," and it calls us to drop into and connect with our inner depth through deep listening. The word *yisrael* means "one who wrestles with God." *Adonai*, or YHVH, means "is-was-will be," and in this prayer, it points to the formless, unmanifest nature of reality. *Eloheinu*, which means "our

God," represents all the forms that manifest in the realm of creation. *Adonai echad* means "all of Being, all of reality is one."

So, this chant is calling us to listen deeply and experience directly that there is no division in the fabric of reality—the inner is the outer, the formless is the form, the transcendent is the immanent, the unmanifest is the manifest, the spiritual is the material, the infinite is the finite—that all is One. What is interesting is that the prayer is actually constructed as if one were saying it to another person, not to God. It's saying something like: "Listen up, you who wrestle with God, we are not separate from each other, we are all one." When considered this way, the *Shema* becomes another tool to help the process of *tikkun*, of repairing the disconnect and fragmentation that we experience in our collective human soul.

So, let's explore this practice through contemplating and chanting this ancient formula. We want to orient to this chant not as a prayer to some distant God, but rather as a call to all the parts within us that feel disconnected and alienated from the whole, from the loving light of spirit, and from the universal human body of light. We are calling upon all the parts within us as well as those within our friends, family, and enemies to "listen up" and remember who they are, to hear the vibrations of oneness that these words carry.

So, begin by finding a comfortable position, and taking a full conscious breath. As you release the breath, also relax and release the thinking mind, dropping into a deeper place. Once you have taken a few full breaths and feel more connected to presence, I suggest that you chant the Hebrew words of the *Shema* several times slowly. You can just recite the words in a monotone or you can allow your inner spirit to generate a spontaneous melody and cadence that feels natural for you. For the purpose of this exercise, it does not matter if you do not pronounce the words correctly; it is the orientation of the heart that is most important.

As you play with this chant, allow the ancient words and the sacred vibrations they carry to touch you. Notice how the words impact your experience and your state of consciousness. When your chanting feels complete, I suggest that you sit in silence for a few minutes, marinating in the presence that has been generated through the practice.

CHAPTER 23

THE SOULSHIP

The *Shema* chant is one expression of the journey of wholeness since it embodies the vibrational transmission of the union of the inner and outer lights, the union of the spiritual and material. It also embodies the collective dimension of the journey of wholeness, which has to do with the integration of all the individual sparks of light into a more coherent and harmonious organism of presence. The *Shema*, therefore, expresses that point of intersection between the vertical and horizontal dimensions of reality, between the universal and individual trees of life.

When our Presence Body (the awakened individual consciousness) succeeds in waking down to free up the inner light at the heart of our contractions, then the Presence Body can manifest into what we call the Pearl Body. This is the complete human being, one who is *tocho kevaro*—one whose inside is like their outside. The Hebrew word for "pearl" is *penina*, which, on the mystical level, signifies the integration of the inside and the outside along with the ten *sefirot*—divine qualities—into the Presence Body in a manner that allows these qualities the freedom to be expressed and lived in everyday life. Thus, in Kedumah, becoming this kind of whole and integrated human being is the mark of true enlightenment. This is reflected in the word "enlightenment" itself, which features the words "ten" and "light" at its center.

This process of integration is reflected in the biblical narrative that we have been tracking. Following the exodus of the Israelites from Egypt, the Torah describes a fifty-day process of what is traditionally called "counting of the *omer*." This ritual, which many still perform, entails counting the days from Passover to the festival of *Shavuot* (sometimes called in English the "Feast of Weeks" or "Pentecost") and celebrating, among other things, the receiving of the Torah on Mount Sinai. Mystically speaking, this period marks a deep-dive waking down process into all the psychological structures that have wired and patterned our thinking mind since childhood.

On each of the first forty-nine days, a different combination of *sefirot* and their corresponding psychological distortions are consciously explored and worked with in order to ground and integrate the waking up experience of Passover into our everyday experience of life. On the fiftieth day (the traditional number that signifies wholeness), the festival of *Shavuot* is celebrated, marking the completion of the process of becoming a fully mature and complete human being—one who is free, autonomous, and deeply connected to the totality.

Through fully experiencing these contracted patterns and fully understanding them in the light of presence, the neuropathways that carry these patterns are rewired from their contracted historical conditioning into more efficient conduits of presence. This is why the Pearl Body, the number fifty, and the completion of this process is associated with the *sefirah* of *binah* ("understanding") in the Tree of Life. It is through inquiry into and deep understanding of our patterns that we become free from them. This is also reflected in the ancient biblical tradition that every fiftieth year, the Jubilee year, all slaves and prisoners are to be freed.

Another significant shift occurs over the course of this fifty-day process, a shift in our relationship with God. On Passover, we relate to God as a parent, as a savior. We scream out to God for help to lift us up out of our pain. However, by the time we reach *Shavuot*, we relate to God as a partner, a lover, an equal. This is why the ancient sages point out that on *Shavuot*, the event at Mount Sinai was really a marriage ceremony between the people and God. The texts state that Mount Sinai was held over the heads of the people like a *chuppah*—a wedding canopy—and the Torah scroll itself is the *ketubah*, the marriage document.

So, we see that only through working through our psychological and emotional issues, through fully experiencing and understanding our contractions, is it possible to become a whole person. And, it is only possible to engage in a real relationship, a true intimate partnership, from a place of personal freedom, autonomy, and wholeness in ourselves.

Through the Pearl Body, we are able to express ourselves in the world—through our actions and interactions with others—in a manner that is real, authentic, and connected to our inner realization of truth. It is also naturally sensitive to other beings and respectful of all life. This development of the journey of wholeness therefore cannot happen in isolation or through meditating in a cave. It can only be realized through living a complete human life by engaging in relationships, community, and the full range of human activities that are available to us.

The journey of wholeness therefore reveals the true nature of the *merkavah* as not only an individual manifestation but also a collective one. In Kedumah we therefore call the more fully realized *merkavah* the Soulship. This has a double meaning, as it points both to its function as an individual vehicle—an inner spaceship of travel and discovery—as well as a communal vehicle—a fellowship of souls—in a conscious process of collective awakening and evolution.

This process is reflected in the ancient Kabbalistic teachings about the meaning of the word *merkavah* itself. As we saw earlier in the course, this word shares its roots with the Hebrew words for *keruvim* (cherubs), and the word *berakha* (blessing), both of which express different dimensions of presence. But the ancient mystics also point out that the word *merkavah* can also mean to "combine" or "graft" together, as in grafting the branches of two trees together. Thus, the mystical function of the *merkavah* includes the practice of grafting the letters of the scroll together to form new combinations of letters and words. This practice was the main meditation technique taught by the famous Kabbalist Abraham Abulafia, and was used to induce prophecy and draw down an influx of divine presence into the body.

When applied through the Kedumah framework, this practice of grafting the letters together is achieved through linking our souls together in interpersonal partner and group inquiry exercises. This reflects the ancient teachings that the letters of the scroll are metaphors for each individual soul. Through our personal inquiry into the truth of our experience in the here and now, and through sharing our process with others, we interpenetrate each other and the essential presence—the ink—of our souls intersects and enriches each other, forming and birthing a new collective human organism of presence in the process. Through combining and connecting with other letters of the scroll, we re-member (that is, put back together) and heal the collective human soul, and in the process, the cosmic Tree of Life is brought back into harmony.

So, take some time to continue to play with the *Shema* practice (see chapter 22). You can try it out in its traditional form by chanting it upon rising and upon going to sleep at night. Or, try it whenever you feel moved to invite its wisdom into your consciousness. Also, try to find as many opportunities as you can to practice speaking and listening to others from a place of presence. These two practices work together to deepen our personal healing and collective journey to freedom.

CHAPTER 24

THE COSMIC WOMB

I n the Hebrew Bible, the journey of wholeness—the fifty days of counting the *omer* between Passover and *Shavuot*—occurs while traveling in the desert. This process of integrating the lights of Being (i.e. the ten *sefirot*) is facilitated through the conscious articulation of our speech, which allows the human consciousness to participate in the expressive effulgence of creation. This is not only reflected in the Hebrew word for "desert," *midbar*, which can also mean "speaking," but also in the Hebrew phrase *sefirat ha-omer*, which is the original designation for the practice of counting of the *omer*.

The word *sefirat* (usually translated as "counting") can also mean "clarification" or "illumination," or it can be a reference to the *sefirot* themselves. Furthermore, the word *omer* (עמר) is pronounced the same (and has a nearly identical spelling) as one of the Hebrew words for "speaking" (אמר). The only difference is that one is spelled with the letter *ayin* and the other with the letter *aleph*. This is similar to the linguistic transformation that we discussed earlier in chapter

11, whereby Adam and Eve's garments of skin are transmuted into garments of light. Therefore, on a deeper level, the practice of *sefirat ha-omer* points to the process of integrating all the *sefirot*—the lights of Being—into one's consciousness through the practice of illuminated speech.

According to the Talmud, during this period of counting the omer between Passover and *Shavuot*, a plague struck and killed 12,000 inquiry pairs in the ancient school of Rabbi Akiva, one of the great heroes of the Jewish tradition. According to the Talmud, these inquiry partners died from a choking disease that affected the throat, the reason being that they did not relate to each other with respect. However, the text can also be translated as "they did not treat each other with presence." This translation difference comes from the Hebrew word *kavod*, which is a common term used both to mean "respect" as well as to be a reference to the divine presence. In this sense, we can understand that the deaths were caused by the fact that they related to each other in a manner that was disconnected from presence.

On the mystical level, this Talmudic story is not meant to be taken literally. Rather, it is meant to communicate a teaching about reality, truth, and human nature. By associating the plague with a choking throat affliction, the Talmud is alluding to the blockage of the throat center which is the anatomical correspondence for *da'at*, intimate knowing, as well as for the capacity for true speech.

The purification process of the counting of the *omer* calls us to integrate our embodied presence and our true speech whenever we relate to others. It calls us to relate to others with the sensitivity and respect that presence carries for all beings, for all life. When we do so, we establish more coherence, integrity, and unification throughout our universal human soul. When we don't, we generate a communal plague as it were, a collective inner state that is akin to death. This is a metaphor for a way of living and relating with each other that is disconnected from the Tree of Life and our true nature.

Engaging this deep process of individual and collective healing opens up the portals to true freedom. This is reflected in the Torah teachings on the Jubilee year (*yovel* in Hebrew), which is celebrated every fiftieth year and is marked by a collective return to origins, including the freeing of all slaves and prisoners. The Kabbalists correlated the Jubilee year with the *sefirah* of *binah*, since it is the divine quality associated with the number fifty and the principle of wholeness.

In this sense, *binah* and wholeness represent a portal into a deeper dimension of freedom than that experienced in the journey of expansion. The freedom experienced in the journey of expansion is always relative to contraction. We can only feel expansive in contrast to feeling contracted, and vice versa. You can't have one without the other. This means that there is always a more hidden underlying contraction at the heart of every expansion, just as there is always a hidden underlying expansion at the heart of every contraction.

This explains why it is the case for many people that experiences of expansion do not bring real freedom. Rather, they oftentimes swing quickly back into contraction, or their realization of expansion is marked by a covert attempt to hold on to the experience or to maintain the state of expansion for as long as possible. This attempt to manipulate their experience is driven by an underlying and more subtle form of suffering: one born out of a deep preference for expansion over contraction and the belief that expansion is "good" and contraction is "bad." Therefore, while the journey of expansion feels spacious and free relative to the experience of contraction, it still carries a certain kind of suffering, one that expresses itself in the desire to avoid the pain of contraction as much as possible.

The experience of the Pearl Body offers a resolution to this split between contraction and expansion since it reveals the integral place that contractions have in our human process of evolution. In the experience of wholeness, we recognize that all our suffering, all of our wounds, all of our personal history, all of our child parts, have meaning and value. We see that they are all equally divine, equally Presence, and as precious and real as is the expansiveness of Being.

Wholeness is thus the embodiment of a total and unconditionally loving inclusivity, it is the wisdom of holding all of our parts in the cosmic womb of life, in the celestial feminine light of *binah*. In the wisdom-womb of *binah*, all of our contradictory parts can coexist and be held simultaneously in the presence of unconditional regard.

In this spirit, the light of *binah* and the principle of wholeness is correlated in the Kabbalah with the process of returning—of *teshuva*—as well as with the *mikvah*, the ritual bath that we discussed earlier in chapter 17. According to this ancient teaching, when we come back into alignment with presence from a place of love of truth for its own sake, when our horizontal and vertical axes sync up, when our inner and outer lights are unified, all of our past misdeeds, mistakes, and misaligned actions are magically transformed into merits on our behalf. They are alchemically transmuted into the essential substance of the ink of our Presence Body, of our individual letter.

The way the Talmud formulates it, all of our past sins are transformed into merits. The word "sin" in this sense should be understood according to its original meaning in the Hebrew as something that "misses the mark"; that is, any behavior that is out of alignment with the truth of presence. This alchemical transmutation is possible because *binah* is the cosmic womb, the source of both the individual and universal communal soul.

So, when we engage the inner-outer journey of wholeness, we are immersing ourselves in the healing waters of the celestial womb. Through the magic of these waters of life, all of our personal history is transformed into the inner organs and cells of a new human being. Just as a pearl is formed over many years through the friction of sand and sea, so too are we slowly born anew through the oftentimes painful friction of our contractions and expansions.

So, let's explore this teaching together with an exercise. First, sense into your inner body and connect to presence. Then, think of a situation in your life that you feel conflicted emotions about or consider contradictory parts at play in your psyche. If you need a minute to find a good example, then just take some time to contemplate the question.

Usually, the tendency when we experience this contradictory set of forces is to want to take one side or other of this polarity. In this simple exercise, just notice what it's like if—instead of trying to figure out which part is right or which is wrong, which is better or which is worse, which is more aligned and which is less aligned—you simply allow both contradictory parts to simultaneously be fully present at the same time, without any fantasy of ever resolving the contradiction for the rest of your life.

See what happens in your embodied experience when you hold your experience in this way. If it helps, you can also journal about your experience or discuss it with an inquiry partner. Between now and whenever you read the next chapter, continue to practice holding your conflicting experience as much as possible in this inclusive manner, without any motivation to fix or change, and notice what you experience.

CHAPTER 25

LOVE AND ONENESS

T he *Shema* chant carries with it a certain quality of transmission, a particular vibration that helps cultivate the embodied experience of wholeness in the soul. It declares, both with its words as well as with its nonconceptual vibrations, that all contradictions are ultimately two sides of one unified reality. This is how the *Shema* chant and the practice of simultaneously holding our contradictory experiences work together and help us shift our perception of reality into a more nondual and inclusive mode.

In this approach, we are actually fusing two methods into one. We are applying the technique of witnessing the content of our experience without identifying with such content, and at the same time, we are invoking the underlying nondual presence of unconditional love. Both of these dimensions of the path are implied in the text of the *Shema* prayer.

Let's look at this more deeply. The *Shema* prayer originally appears as a verse in the book of Deuteronomy. The last word of the verse, *echad*, which means "one," is immediately followed by the word *ve-ahavta*, which means "and you shall love," from the Hebrew word *ahavah*, meaning "love." The principle of *ahavah* thus appears in the Torah immediately following that of *echad*—the two words are literally right next to each other. So when you read the text, you could read it as *echad-ahavah*, which means "one-love." This principle is also reflected in the fact that the *gematria*—numerical value—of the Hebrew word love, *ahavah*, is thirteen, which is also the numeric value as the Hebrew word one, *echad*. So, there is an intimate relationship between these two principles.

When we experience wholeness, we are feeling the effects of the boundless dimension of divine love, which is the cosmic force that births the embodied Pearl. This expression of love displays itself specifically as constituting everything; our entire field of perception is colored by this love. Love is thus the gateway from wholeness to oneness and is its defining feature. In the Hebrew mystical tradition, this quality of boundless love is correlated with the principle of grace. The Hebrew word for "grace" is *chayn*, and it consists of two letters, *chet* and *nun*. If you reverse the letters and spell it backward, you get *nun* and *chet*, which spells *nach* and means "rest."

When we experience divine love, the soul is profoundly impacted by the sense that it can finally rest. We feel that we can finally settle deeply. We know with absolute certainty that we are indeed held in love, that we are intrinsically and inherently worthy of love. Not only are we worthy of it, but it is here for us; we are swimming in it and it is available to us personally. The transformative moment occurs when we feel this love and know it in our body-soul.

In this presence of love, the soul can finally let go, rest, and abide in its center. So much of our inability to rest and abide in the center is because we are not feeling this unconditional love. With this one-love, we can rest undisturbed even if we are experiencing contradictory feelings. It shifts our baseline from one of dis-ease to one of stillness and peace. Then, rather than imprisoning us, our contracted experiences become an organic part of the whole constellation of forces at play in our totality.

When we realize that there is nothing we need to do to be loved by God then it is possible for us to drop into a deep state of rest or repose. With divine love and grace, we can finally drop into the depths, into the center. When we allow this to happen, then we are turning more toward the still, silent, and dimensionless ground of Being. Thus, the realization that all is constituted by love is the doorway from the journey of wholeness (marked by speech and words) to the journey of vastness (constituted by the primordial sounds, the vowel sounds that animate the words, and the all-penetrating presence of stillness and silence).

The *Shema* prayer also holds within it a second hidden teaching that has to do with the inner movement from the journey of wholeness to that of vastness. If you look inside a traditional Torah scroll, you will see that there are two Hebrew letters in the *Shema* verse that are bigger than all the others. There is a big letter *ayin* in the word *shema*, and there is a big letter *dalet* at the end of the word *echad*. When read in order of appearance in the text, these two letters spell *ayd*, which means "witness." If you read it in reverse order, they spell *da*, which means "know," the imperative form of the word *da'at*.

So, we see that the primary contemplative prayer of the ancient Hebrew tradition calls us not only to perceive and experience oneness and love, but it also alludes to a technique of how to achieve this, through a hidden play on words. By highlighting the letters *ayin* and *dalet* in the *Shema*, the Torah is alluding to how this method—the witness practice—can be a bridge to the nondual experience, to the true knowledge that is carried in the vibrations of the *Shema*.

Now, let's move into exploring a new practice, the *ayd* practice, or witness practice. Earlier, we explored the contemplative practice of speaking the truth. This foundational practice is necessary before we can fully appreciate and taste the fruits of the *ayd* practice. This progression is reflected in the verse from Proverbs: "True speech will be established forever." However, this verse can also be translated as: "True speech will establish the witness." This is because the last word, *le-ad*—meaning "forever"—can also be read *le-ayd*, meaning "witness." So, on this path, we first work with the practice of speaking the truth, which then establishes the possibility for the *ayd* practice to bear its fruits so we can more readily integrate them into our everyday life.

There are five steps to the *ayd* practice. The first is to notice, be aware, and witness the content of our sense perceptions. In this step, we watch all phenomena: thoughts, emotions, breath, and sensations. We assume an inner posture of bearing witness to whatever is arising in our experience.

The second step is to become aware of the spaces between and around the content. This entails noticing the spaces between the sounds and the words, between the breaths, between the thoughts, and the spaces around the objects we see.

The third step is to become aware of both the content of our experience as well as the spaces around and between the content, all at the same time.

The fourth step is to become aware of the experiencing consciousness itself, to become aware of that which is aware along with the various contents of our experience. As we establish our awareness of the witness, there will start to be moments in which the witness, the observer, itself falls away. There will be gaps and spaces that arise where no observer can be found.

The fifth step is to be present and aware in these gaps, in the spaces in which no witness and no observer can be found. At this stage of the practice, the knower and the known effortlessly become one. There is no longer any witness and no longer anything being witnessed. There is simply witnessing happening: pure awareness, without a subject or an object. This is the nondual *echad*—the ultimate oneness of Being—that is the promise of the *Shema*.

So, let's explore this practice by using a visual object, but it can be done with any external or internal sense perception. Have a look around and notice what you perceive in your environment. You will likely see images of various objects. Choose one object, any object. Notice the object. Notice its color, shape, texture.

Now, also notice the space around it.

Now, include in your awareness both the object and the space around it at the same time.

Next, notice the experiencing consciousness itself, the one who is observing the object and the space around the object.

As you maintain your awareness of the witnessing consciousness, notice any gaps or moments where the witness itself falls away. Turn toward those gaps, those spaces, and be aware and awake.

If you step fully into this practice, you will start to notice everything melding into a unified field of perception, without a distinct observer or an observed. This is the nondual state of oneness.

If you move deeper into these gaps of the witness, you will start to experience an erasure of the thinking mind. It can feel as if in an instant, everything goes blank. This is the doorway to the blank parchment of the scroll, the primordial mystery of deep stillness and silence, and our eternal home.

CHAPTER 26

THE SOUNDS
OF SILENCE

We've been learning how speech functions as a practice to bring us more in contact with the substance of the soul, with the ink of the letter. It does this by filling out the horizontal axis of both the individual and collective dimensions of the human soul. In this process of the journey of wholeness, the unification of the inner and outer lights of Being—the vertical and horizontal axes, or the inner and outer expressions of our individual life—come into harmony, integration, and fulfillment.

As we fill in and fill out our individual and collective presence, we invite more and more of the boundless quality of love into our consciousness, which then allows us to rest and drop more deeply into our inner space. In this deepening process, our perception begins to open to the journey of vastness, which correlates with the sefirah of *chochmah*, the realm of primordial wisdom in the Kabbalistic teachings of the Tree of Life.

In this dimension, we come to appreciate more directly the profound silence and stillness that is at the very heart of all experience and all phenomena. In this state, silence and stillness is all-pervading and does not depend on the absence of noise or sound. That is, the presence of stillness and silence is palpably felt and experienced even as other content—including sounds—appear in our field of perception.

Getting in touch with this stillness brings profound peace to the soul and really shifts our journey and experience of everyday life in remarkable ways. We begin to see that it is possible to abide in the deep peace of inner silence even in the presence of pain, suffering, and whatever external chaos may be happening in our environment.

We have been cultivating our capacity to be aware of this dimension of experience from the very beginning of this book. In the first practice, we consciously began including and being present to the silence and stillness between the words and between the breaths. Through this practice, we start to experience the spaces between the words and breaths as the unchanging ground underlying all the content of our experience.

From this inner space, we can discern that the world of appearances is an expression of the primordial divine speech, of the innermost sounds of creation, of the vibrations that emanate from the hidden mystery of the infinite. It is even possible to experience in the depths of this silence a different order of sound altogether—primordial sounds, the ancient hums of the recondite source of Being prior to its becoming in the process of creation. These sounds are the primal forces of creation, the spirits that animate the divine speech through which reality comes into form. These sounds are the sounds of silence.

According to the Kabbalah, while the words and the letters derive from the cosmic womb (what is known in Kabbalah as the *sefirah* of *binah* and in Kedumah as the journey of wholeness), the vowel sounds themselves derive from *chochmah*, the primordial ground of wisdom and creation, what we call the journey of vastness.

All twenty-two letters of the Hebrew language are consonants. So, all the words and all the letters are animated by this more primordial expression of sound, the vowel sounds themselves. The vowels are implicit in the words; they represent a more primordial dimension prior to manifestation of form. It is the dimension of the divine voice out of which the speech of creation flows.

This hidden source is the timeless mystery of the journey of vastness, which is the source of the individual consciousness and the created realm. This primordial ground of creation expresses itself through the seed syllables of the vowel sounds. So, when we chant and invoke the vowel sounds, we are really inviting into our experience the primordial roots of our consciousness, the inner nature of our Being.

So, let's explore this teaching more deeply through embodying it in a practice. In this practice, which is derived from an ancient Kabbalistic meditation, I invite you to chant the five primary Hebrew vowel sounds. These vowel sounds are: *oh, ah, ay, ee, oo.* I suggest that you extend each vowel for a length of time, and then repeat the sequence of five vowels several times.

As you chant, be as embodied and present with your experience as possible. Allow the sounds, and the vibrations they carry, to touch you. Notice how they affect you and your state of consciousness. Also, see if you can notice the presence of silence and stillness that abides at the center of these primordial sounds. When your practice comes to a natural conclusion, just sit for a few moments in silence, absorbing the presence generated by the practice.

CHAPTER 27

A STAR IS BORN

The inner journey into deeper states of silence and stillness brings us to a realm beyond the thinking mind, beyond speech and words, beyond all that is known. When we approach this inner depth from a place of wholeness, then we can be in deep stillness and silence while remaining in the world, even as we are no longer of the world.

As children, we learn to focus all of our attention on all the noise, content, and material of our inner and outer world: on our thinking, our emotions, our sensations, our identities, and all of the external objects and sense-stimulants that capture our attention throughout each day. This is what we have been calling the journey of contraction.

In the journeys of expansion and wholeness, our awareness begins to include the gaps and spaces between the content of our experience as well as the experiencing consciousness itself. In the journey of vastness, the focus of our awareness and interest shifts to the gaps and spaces of the witness itself, to those moments where the witness falls away revealing the mystery of no-content, no-self, and no-mind.

In this more profound turn inward, we discover that the gaps between the words, breaths, and thoughts, and ultimately, the gaps in our sense of our perceiving consciousness itself, are not confined or limited to the locations in time and space in which we first access them. The stillness that is present in the space of no-self, in the blank mind, in the blank parchment of the scroll is also present at the heart of every single word, every single breath, every single thought of our entire consciousness.

The blank mind of silence, stillness, and peace is the ground of all the content of our experience, just as the blank parchment is the ground of all the letters and words that appear upon the scroll. This ground is always-already present in the here-now of each and every moment. In the journey of vastness, we begin to feel the deep peace of presence not just in the spaces in between the mundane content of our lives, but we begin to feel it as the ground of everything that is happening all the time, as the ground of our very being.

Right now, as you read these words, see what it's like to just be here without doing anything at all. If there is thinking happening, then just notice the thoughts and allow them as you also include the spaces between the thoughts. Now, also be aware of the experiencing consciousness itself, the ink that is animating your letter. As you sense your embodied presence and are simultaneously aware of the one who is aware, notice any gaps where the experiencing consciousness falls away. Settle into these mind gaps, into these blank spaces. Notice what arises in this state of just being.

Now, allow yourself to drop into the depth of these spaces, into the deep darkness of its waters. Allow yourself to descend into the dense waters of Being. In these depths, the mind becomes quiet—there is no thinking, just more and more presence of pure nothingness, of emptiness, of blankness. You may start to feel as if you are immersed in the deep, dark waters of the ocean, far from the surface above. Or, it may feel as if you are surrounded by the deep, dark space of the vast night sky.

Allow your body to absorb this dense, black presence of silence and stillness as if the cells of your body were being saturated by this dense substance of complete peace. Feel the bliss of your body absorbing these still waters. In this profound state of silence, stillness, and deep peace, you will begin to experience a scintillating point of light, a star shining at the very center of all things, at the center of your being. A timeless, dimensionless star of light is discovered to be eternally shining in the vastness of inner space.

This star and the light that it emanates—the starlight—is the first light. It is the original primordial light of creation and the first light of our individual soul. It is what we always were, always are, and always will be. As the star of light, we are eternally shining, whether we are alive or dead, whether we have a body or no longer have a body. When our thinking mind is erased in the waters of silence, we transcend all the dichotomies of the conceptual mind, including the concepts of life and death.

In this nonconceptual mode of experiencing, we discover our true individual nature as timeless and deathless. In this state, we realize that we were never born and that we will never die. This state is the return to the primordial Eden, to our original deathless nature, to the cosmic interface between the infinite and the finite, to the source of reality.

With this discovery comes a new kind of freedom, the freedom from life and death, the freedom from having to be somebody who we are not. With the discovery of the star of light we have discovered our true eternal self, we know without any doubt that our essence can never be lost or destroyed. We finally know directly who we really are, and with this knowledge comes an unspeakable peace and freedom.

In the Kabbalah, this discovery of the true self, of the original light of consciousness, is correlated with the *sefirah* of *chochmah*, of wisdom. In the Zohar, it is called the *nekudah*, which means the "point," referring to the point of light that is the first light of creation and the most primordial expression of the individual soul. It is also called the "star," reflecting how it can be experienced as a star of light shining in vast, black, inner space.

There is a verse in the Torah that states: "And a star shall go forth." The ancient commentaries explain that this is a reference to the messiah, who appears in the form of a star of light. When understood mystically, every human being is a potential messiah; we each have the potential to discover our true nature as this primordial star of light.

In the last chapter, we explored vowel sounds as the cosmic precursors to the created realm of form, as the primordial roots of our individual consciousness. This relates to the revelation of the point of light as the first light of consciousness since traditionally, the vowel sounds are symbolized in the Hebrew language with points— dots above, beneath, and within the letters. This correlates with the primordial light of vastness that surrounds and fills us, that is within and without us. So, the vowel sounds and the point of light share a common origin: the cosmic seed of creation prior to its gestation and birth in the cosmic womb of life.

The star of light can manifest as a distinct point or as a clear, open, vast, nondual space. Because the point is nondimensional, its nondual light can therefore shine in any form, as a concentrated point or as vast, clear openness. The chief characteristic of the star of light and the vastness of omnipresent nondual light is pure Being. The wisdom of the star of light is that there is nothing that we can do to be what we are. We are always what we were, always what we are, and always what we will be. And there is nothing we can do to be or not be that.

So, there is no practice that we can do to become this point of light. We already are that. The journey of vastness thus has to do with integrating the wisdom of just being, the wisdom of not doing anything at all to alter the simplicity of what we are.

So, see what it's like to play with the sense of just being throughout your day. Notice what you experience and how you feel when you just are your true self, a star of light eternally shining in the vastness of infinite space.

CHAPTER 28

THE BLACK LIGHT

The star of light, our eternal true self, reveals itself to us when we fully drop down into the depths of our being. When we totally surrender to the unknown, the witnessing consciousness itself falls away. In this state of no-mind and no-self, we are able to perceive how it is that our innermost nature, the original light of our primordial Being, always-already was, is, and will-be shining in the vastness of our inner-outer space.

The backdrop of our star of light, our true self, is thus the deep, black space of pure nothingness. In the depths of this mysterious nothingness, all friction and agitation in the nervous system are erased. All thinking and all experiential content, both inner and outer, are silenced. All that is left is a palpable nothingness, a dense, black space so still and silent that not a single ripple can be discerned.

The Kabbalists call this *ayin*, which means "nothingness." This word is one of the code terms for the uppermost *sefirah* in the Tree of Life, usually called *keter*, which means "crown." This is the dimension of what the Zohar calls in Aramaic the *botzina de-kardenuta*, the primordial black luminosity of absolute nothingness. In this state, there is the cessation of all phenomena, of all thinking. With the annihilation of the thinking mind, there is also the erasure of not only the conventional sense of self, but also of all sense of self whatsoever, even the true eternal self, the primordial star of light.

According to the Hebrew mystics, when we plant a seed in the earth, in order for it to grow it first must completely dissolve into nothing. Then, from nothingness, life sprouts forth. This is called in Aramaic the *kusta de-chiyuta*—the "remnant of life." The remnant of life is the seed that sprouts out of complete nothingness. The seed is a reference to the point of light, which correlates in Kabbalah to the sefirah of *chochmah*, primordial wisdom. Experientially, we must therefore completely dissolve into nothingness—a condition of no-self—in order for the first light of our Being to shine forth.

Another way this process is depicted in the ancient texts is through a play on words. The Hebrew word for "I"—the sense of self—is *ani*. If you rearrange the Hebrew letters of this word, you get *ayin*, which means "nothingness." This process of transforming the *ani*—the somebody—into the *ayin*—the nobody, the nothingness—reflects the inner transformation of identifying with having a self to the realization of no-self.

The black light of nothingness is experienced very differently than the vastness of the starlight. Black space has density to it; it can feel like the presence of concentrated space saturates the consciousness and completely erases everything. This does not make sense to the conventional mind because it is both dense and at the same time infinitely vast. It is experienced as an intense negative light, as if its luminosity comes from its radical absence and emptiness. It completely annihilates all concepts of the mind and brings a cessation to all thoughts and to the sense of self. It erases all concepts, all self, all body, and all of the world. It erases everything. The black light annihilates all of reality, including the star and the starlight.

Its effect on the nervous system is one of deep bliss. There can be the sense that the nervous system and the cells of the body are saturated in the dense presence of stillness. We experience our flesh and bones more intensely and palpably than ever, as if our very cells are infused with the nectar of pure bliss. If you drop down into the core of your being right now, you may be able to sense it.

As I write these words right now, everything around me is absorbed in this dense, black space. Wherever you are right now, everything surrounding you is saturated in this sublime, mysterious, black depth. Sense into it. Sense into its stillness, its silence, its mystery that is everywhere and permeating everything. The black, dense light impacts us with a profound sense of stillness and silence. The primordial nothingness of reality abides undisturbed in the midst of the hustle and bustle of life.

There are two different facets to the journey of vastness. The first facet is the star of light itself, which can manifest either as a distinct point of timeless, dimensionless light, or it can appear as the vast starlight itself, as the primordial first light of creation that permeates everything. The second facet to the journey of vastness is the backdrop of black luminosity, the ground of absolute mystery out of which the star of light emerges to reveal its presence, its starlight.

For me and many of my students, the journey of vastness oftentimes reveals itself in a manner that includes both of these facets at the same time: as a bright star shining in the deep, black, silent inner night. In this experience, the black luminosity correlates with the blank parchment of the scroll while the point of light correlates with the vowel sounds and the vowel points—the seed syllables and dots from which speech and the letters of the scrolls emanate.

When we experience both the starlight and the black light—both the brightness and blank depth of the journey of vastness—then we open up the possibility of an even more radical discovery. Since the black space of *keter*, the crown, is more fundamental and primordial than the point of light, then it is possible for the point itself to be erased by the black light. So, the black light is a deeper level of emptiness that can annihilate even the true-self of the point.

This reveals that there are several layers to the spiritual function of the black light. Firstly, it serves to help expose and erase the conventional sense of self, the conditioned self-identity. This erasure then allows the true self, the spark of light of *chochmah*, to arise in the vastness of this black space. This is the primordial seed of our individual consciousness, the original primordial spark of our soul. Secondly, it functions to annihilate all sense of self whatsoever, including the essential self of the point of light.

This is the deeper meaning of the central Kabbalistic teaching of what is called in Hebrew *bittul hayesh*—meaning the "nullification of something," which is a code term for the erasure of the point of light. Only when the point of light is erased through its absorption into the deep inner space of the black luminosity is the innermost essence of God and of reality available to us. This points to the experience of the deepest realization of the dimension of *keter*, of the hidden crown of consciousness. Here lies the recognition of the absolute nothingness that is the source of all "something," the primordial ground of all creation, the blank parchment of the scroll, and our innermost home of true peace.

CHAPTER 29

THE JOURNEY
OF FREEDOM

As the dense, black light establishes itself in our consciousness and we allow more and more the experience of no-
self, a more radical kind of emptiness or nothingness
can begin to reveal itself. This kind of emptiness is difficult—if not
impossible—to talk about because it is so radical that the words
"emptiness" and "nothingness" do not really even apply to it. It is
not really emptiness or nothingness, because these words are saying
way too much.

I use the word "nothing" because I do not know what else to call
it; hence the additional attribute "radical" to signify that it is not
akin to the nothingness experienced in the journey of vastness or
to that of the black space. The word "nothingness" describes something; it is a concept. However, radical nothingness or emptiness is
so nonconceptual that both the words "nothingness" and "nonconceptual" do not apply to it.

This radical nothingness is the inner essence of the sefirah of *keter*, the crown of consciousness, and it points to the truth of *Ein Sof*, which means "no-end." *Ein Sof* is put in the negative because it is a reality that the Kabbalists intentionally did not talk about. All they can say about it is what it is not, so they say it has "no end." There is nothing you can say about it because actually nothing can be said about it. I am not saying this poetically or metaphorically. There is actually nothing to talk about because there is nothing there. There is no experience of *Ein Sof* that can be described.

Usually, people translate *Ein Sof* into the English word "infinite." However, the word literally means "no-end." *Ein Sof* is not really infinite—it is neither infinite nor is it finite. But at the same time, it is also not not-infinite nor is it not-finite. It is nothing and everything, and it is also not nothing and not everything. It is "neither-nor" and "both-and" as well as not "neither-nor" and "both-and." And even this is not it, because it is not an "it." Since it is not an experience and it is not a thing that exists, then to describe it is impossible. This is why it's not really possible to talk about this kind of emptiness without sounding nonsensical.

In order to talk about this condition of radical emptiness, it may be more useful to discuss the implications of it, to describe its impact on life or our perception of reality. This is how emptiness—on this radical level of which I am speaking—leads to radical freedom. The impact of it on our consciousness is one of equalization of all experience and all phenomena. That is to say, when we perceive reality through the lens of this radical freedom, there is truly no longer a spiritual journey because there is nothing more that can be called "spiritual."

From the perspective of freedom, there is nothing that is more or less spiritual than anything else. In this mode of experience, all that exists is literally what is right in front of our faces. The bare naked simplicity of what I am seeing or doing right now is all there is. There is nothing else. This is literally it. And this "it" is not anything at all that can be held onto or grasped.

So, you can see that the implications of this kind of emptiness are quite radical. It is radical because it reveals that there is a way of experiencing that is so unhinged and unglued from all concepts—from all imprints of the thinking mind—that it reflects a truth that is inconceivable. It is the truth of hyper literal reality, where there is no reference point and no directionality whatsoever. Since there are no abstract or theoretical coordinates, there is nothing outside of the literal factuality of immediate perception.

The journey of freedom is thus not about the freedom to do something or to be something nor is it freedom from something. Rather, it involves the realization that at the heart of it all, we are always-already free from all conceptual categories altogether. It is freedom from the dichotomies of conceptual and nonconceptual, of spirituality and materiality, and even freedom from the concept of freedom itself. It is freedom from the fantasy that there is anything other than what is right here in front of our faces in the right here and the right now.

Thus, the journey of freedom is not about realizing a new dimension of reality or a new state of being, discovering a new aspect of the soul or of a quality of essence. It is not freedom in the sense of having any particular experience of freedom (such as we experience when we move from contraction to expansion). The radical freedom of this journey is quite different because it is not about any particular experience at all. It is more about the way that we are orienting and relating to all the particulars of our experience. In the journey of freedom, all the particulars of our experience, all the content—whether it be a contraction or some kind of state of bliss or expansion—are all recognized as equally valid expressions of the totality.

On the path of the five journeys of Kedumah, first, we experience reality through the filter of the journey of contraction. Then, we wake-up into the journey of expansion, which offers a welcome contrast to contraction. Next, the experiences of contraction and expansion integrate and we wake down into the journey of wholeness. Then, the primordial light of the journey of vastness reveals itself to us, and through its mysterious depths, the portals to the journey of freedom open up. We then unwittingly arrive back at the mundane experience of contraction once again, only this time, our experience of contraction—as well as that of expansion, wholeness, and vastness—is divested of all its psychic charge.

Of course, the path does not always unfold in such a linear manner. It certainly may zig-zag through the five journeys in all kinds of nonlinear ways. But in the journey of freedom, the full range of spiritual experience is available to our consciousness. It is marked by a notable and miraculous absence of psychic and energetic investment in the content of our experience. In this state, there is a constant and undisturbed baseline of emptiness of self, regardless of the particular content of our experience. This state is difficult to describe because it is so radically simple and unremarkable yet totally miraculous at the same time. It's miraculous in its utter simplicity.

Someone who is abiding in this mode of freedom will not think to write home about it. It would, in fact, never occur to them that anything significant is happening. They are in such a natural state that everything flows without effort or intention. They are so simple and content with the ordinary facets of life that in their invisibility and simplicity, they are often missed by the spiritual seekers looking to experience the highs of expansion.

Thus, the impact of the journey of freedom is that we become totally mundane, ordinary, practical. We are interested in whatever is most real in the moment: the food, the weather, or the cosmic and sublime, if that is what is present and relevant. This is what I mean when I say that the spiritual journey itself is over. It is like there are no more spiritual aspirations in the journey of freedom because there is nothing else to seek. What is right in front of our face is more than enough.

It's not that the journey of life is over, because life has really only just begun. But the journey of seeking some ultimate truth is over. Whatever is right in front of us, whatever is most mundane, practical, and down-to-earth, becomes as ultimate as the vastness of space—it is as meaningful as the most sublime experiences of inner bliss.

In the journey of freedom, doing nothing at all is quite fine—in fact, it is endlessly fulfilling. Doing all kinds of activities can also be endlessly fulfilling. We simply do or don't do whatever is natural without any self-consciousness about it. One way I like to describe this condition of freedom is that it is like a zero-calorie beverage: fulfilling and tasty but without any calories. The content of life no longer sticks to us or leaves any trace, but we still engage, appreciate, and learn from it all as it passes by.

There are no formal practices associated with the journey of freedom because any practice or no practice at all is equally applicable depending on what is most natural and effortless. It is the path or the journey of living a frictionless life, of living according to one's natural intelligence. Freedom is thus the fruition of all the practices and of all the journeys. It is the realization of the promise of the spiritual journey: the freedom to be who and what we are without any effort. So, see if between now and when you read the next chapter you can notice what it's like if you allow yourself to just settle into your natural rhythm, into your natural flow of ordinary life.

CHAPTER 30

THE TOTALITY

The journey of freedom frees us from all concepts of spirituality and enlightenment. It's freedom from having to be enlightened. It's freedom to just be an ordinary person—a broken, messed up person. A person with essential light, a person with a history. Everything is totally, radically equalized—the most profound experiences of realization and the most mundane particulars of life.

There is no preference or value as one experience being higher or better than any other. This is what I mean by "radical." It is incomprehensible to our spiritually obsessed identities. In this mode of experience, everything is just exactly what it is, just what is right in front of our face. It is all quite ordinary. I know this may sound like a buzz-kill, but it is really just the erasure of everything that is not needed. There is the sense that there is nothing added and nothing taken away from the experience of life. Everything is just right. It is so authentically what it is.

This is what we mean by the equalization of experience. Having an egoic reaction or an experience of contraction from this perspective is an equally valid expression of reality as is having an experience of black, dense nothingness. Thus, what is usually considered to be enlightenment on the spiritual journey—awakening, presence, expansion—is exposed in the freedom condition as equalized with contraction, limitation, and suffering.

So, it is really the freedom to be both a human being—an ordinary human being, with all of our wounds, contractions, reactions, and all of that—as well as simultaneously a magical being, an embodiment of the cosmic realms of celestial vastness. This mode of experiencing is the embodiment of the totality of the scroll, as it includes all facets of human and cosmic experience as a singular truth, a radically inseparable unity.

In Kedumah, even though we are holding the view of the journey of freedom from the very beginning of the path, we still go through the steps of the five journeys, doing our practices and our personal work. We engage the first four journeys of healing and self-discovery to expand the range of our experience and our perception of reality. This allows for more fruition of freedom in our everyday life.

Also, when we approach the first four journeys from the freedom perspective, the process is more fun, simple, and down-to-earth. With the freedom view, we can be real about what is happening and hold it all with lightness, because, with the erasure of hierarchy, we are less invested in the particular content of our experience. Everything is an expression of the singular truth. So, whatever comes our way, whether it be contraction, reaction, or some kind of bliss, it is just as real and ordinary—and as magical—as any other experience.

This way of experiencing reality is really a necessary portal for appreciating and experiencing more fully the most hidden and invisible mysteries of reality, the most profound secrets of *Ein Sof*. The Kabbalists call this nondimensional portal into the mystery of *Ein Sof* the domain of *yechidah*, which means "singularity." With the recognition of the radical singularity of the scroll, we also realize that every particular of our experience is itself an expression of the totality. Whatever particular is right in front of our face at any moment contains every other particular in reality. Literally everything is in everything. Every particular that ever was, is, and will be is in each and every other particular that ever was, is, and will be.

This is the metaphysical reason for how the process of waking down works, and it also explains why it is that any experience of contraction can be a portal to deeper states of Being and expansion. By fully entering into any experience, even one of contraction and suffering, we unwittingly touch into the totality. Thus, when seen through this lens, the most mundane experiences of life can be portals to the most sublime dimensions of reality. Because every experience contains within it the totality, there is also no end to the journey of revelation and discovery. This no-end, the endless unfolding of realization that is available in every moment and in every experience, is the truth of *Ein Sof*; it is the no-end of reality's possibilities.

The implications of this realization are enormous because it means that everything that ever was, is, and will be is right here and right now. In the journey of freedom, this kind of perception begins to open up more clearly. Basically, the nondimensional truth of the journey of freedom collapses all concepts of distance. It erases the concept that there is distance between moments in time or between points in space or between particular people. So, you can have experiences like being somebody else, being an animal, or being somewhere else in a different time and place. But, it is not that you are journeying somewhere else; it is all happening right here. Everything happens in parallel but interpenetrating realities.

One of the classical Hebrew names for God is *ha-makom*, which means "the place." This divine name reflects this principle that all of existence is a singularity operating in a singular location. There is only one place—one *makom*—where reality manifests; everything that transpires in existence occurs within this singular place. Since there is only one place, this means that there is actually no distance between any two points in existence. Since we are all located in the same singular location, every single point contains every single other point in creation. This is the meaning of the statement in the Talmud that "one who saves a single life saves the entire universe."

At this level of the journey of freedom, our understanding of processes like reincarnation begins to change. The process of birth, death, and rebirth appear differently. It does not make sense from the freedom perspective that we die and are reborn in another body—that we live in a particular body at one point in time and then live in another body at another point in time. From the nondimensional, nondirectional, freedom perspective, we are living in many bodies simultaneously. All times and all places are ever-present in the singularity. There is no past or future life that is dissociated from the singularity, from the one place of existence. It is all just life—the one life of reality of which we are each a living cell that contains all cells.

This also explains how in the journey of freedom, radical differences can coexist without friction and how contradictory truths can simultaneously be present. This is reflected in the Talmudic principle of *elu v'elu divrei elohim chayyim*, which means: "These words and those words are both the words of the living God." This principle allows for radical diversity of views, experiences, and truths to be equal expressions of the totality, even if they contradict each other. The freedom truth thus equalizes and harmonizes difference without diminishing or whitewashing the radical differences that display themselves upon the scroll of the totality.

This is why in the very first chapter I quoted the ancient *Book of Creation* where it states: "The end is embedded in the beginning and the beginning is embedded in the end." We began this book with the teaching on how the journey of freedom (the end) and the journey of contraction (the beginning) are embedded in one another and interpenetrate with each other. The entire perspective of Kedumah is based on this understanding.

That is also why, when we do our interpersonal practices together, we are simultaneously separate and particularized people inquiring together, and, at the same time, we each contain the totality and thoroughly interpenetrate each other. We thus honor and celebrate radical difference even as we participate in the shared embodiment of the singularity of creation, of the scroll. The freedom truth allows for this radical paradox of the particular and the universal to simultaneously coexist.

This concludes our exploration of the Path of Primordial Light. Thank you for joining me on this journey of awakening, of presence, and of freedom. May these teachings and practices be a blessing for each one of you. And may these blessings touch all beings across all dimensions and all realities that are forever present in the eternal here and now.

ABOUT THE AUTHOR

ZVI ISH-SHALOM, PHD, is a professor of wisdom traditions at Naropa University and is the guiding teacher of Kedumah, the Primordial Transmissions, and the Soulship. His previous books include *The Kedumah Experience: The Primordial Torah* and *Sleep, Death, and Rebirth: Mystical Practices of Lurianic Kabbalah.*

For more information about the author and his work, visit: **primordialight.com**.